ON THE ROAD TO PERFECTION

GEORGE MALONEY

ON THE ROAD TO PERFECTION

Christian Humility in Modern Society

NEW CITY PRESS

Dedicated to
Debbie O'Connor, her parents, Marian and Mike,
and their other children, Rosemary, Billy and Michael,
who learned humility the old-fashioned way.

Sincere thanks to
Cyndy and Bill Murphy, Ray Miles,
and Sister Rita for their help.

New City Press, 202 Cardinal Rd., Hyde Park, NY 12538
©1995 George Maloney
Printed in the United States of America

Imprimi Potest:
Bert R. Thelen, S.J.
Provincial of the Society of Jesus
Wisconsin Province

Library of Congress Cataloging-in-Publication Data:

Maloney, George A., 1924-
   On the road to perfection : Christian humility in modern society
/ George Maloney.

   Includes bibliographical references.
   ISBN 1-56548-035-X
   1. Humility—Christianity. 2. Spiritual life—Catholic Church.
  3. Catholic Church—Doctrines. I. Title.
BV4647.H8M35   1995
241'.4—dc20   95-16785

Scripture quotations are taken with permission from the publishers:
The Jerusalem Bible, ©1966 Darton, Longman & Todd and Doubleday &
Co., Inc. and *Good News for Modern Man: The New Testament in Today's Eng-
lish Version,* ©1966 The American Bible Society.

Contents

Introduction

Imagine that Jesus were to return in the flesh today. What advice do you think he would give us to change our chaotic, self-centered lives and to seriously listen to his voice in our hearts?

He never gave us a blueprint or a detailed rule of life, which would guarantee us to be saved if we obeyed it to the letter. When we look at the great saints of the Church, we find that many did not preach the gospel in foreign lands, as Paul, Peter and the early apostles did. Some fasted and lived very demanding, ascetical lives like the Fathers and Mothers of the desert. Other saints were not able to do much fasting or to devote long hours to praying unceasingly (1 Th 5:17). Some saints were virgins, others were married. Some were popes, others were laypersons. Some were intellectual giants and great scholars, others were very simple, even uneducated persons.

But there has never been a holy Christian person, who did not feel that he or she had to live a humble life as Jesus did. All saints sought to obey Jesus who commands us even today: "Learn of me, for I am gentle and humble of heart" (Mt 11:29). I am thoroughly convinced that Jesus would teach us this command again and again, and have us practice it diligently. This would be a sign of our fidelity to him; a sign of our courage to be his disciples, and to become truly human, joyful and creative persons.

The self-emptying Christ

When we prayerfully contemplate the earthly life of Jesus as it is presented in the gospels, we are moved deeply by the depths of his humility. Paul summarizes how we are to imitate the attitude that guided Jesus in his mission among us:

> The attitude you should have is the one that Christ
>   Jesus had:
> He always had the very nature of God,
> But he did not think that by force he should try to become
>   equal with God.
> Instead, of his own free will he gave it all up,
> And took the nature of a servant.
> He became like man, he appeared in human likeness;
> He was humble and walked the path of obedience
>   to death—his death on the cross.
> For this reason God raised him to the highest place above,
> And gave him the name that is greater than any other
>   name.
>
> (Philippians 2:5-9)

Here we have God incarnate showing us that he is the highest in power, holiness, beauty and wisdom; yet out of love for us he became the lowest. He lived out, "what seems to be God's foolishness is wiser than men's wisdom, and what seems to be God's weakness is stronger than men's strength" (1 Co 1:25). For this reason Augustine exhorts Christians of all times to come to Jesus and learn humility from his teaching and example:

> O Teacher and Lord of mortals, unto whom death was pledged and passed on in the cup of pride, he would not teach what he himself was not. He would not bid what he himself did not. I see you, O good Jesus, with the eyes of faith which you have opened for me, as in an assembly of the human race, crying out and saying, "Come unto me, and learn of me."[1]

Self-sufficiency

But why do we moderns think so rarely of humility and have such little desire to practice it in our daily lives? We have lost our sense of belonging to a community, not only in our families, but also in our parishes, in religious orders, in our neighborhoods, at work, in our nation and in the entire universe. We have rejected historical traditions, and therefore we disregard our need to belong to a community based on traditional values handed down by our ancestors. We tend to perceive ourselves as rugged individuals, not in need of any community. Through our Western culture each of us has become "an island unto ourselves," as the poet John Donne wrote.

Our own ideas, longings, ambitions and beliefs have no connection to a historical community larger than ourselves. *I* decide what is important, moral and truthful. It is the way *I* see things that makes everything correct and truthful. How difficult it is in such a culture to think of the virtue of humility as anything other than a repressing of our human nature![2]

Ted Turner, owner of CNN Broadcasting, explains his personal philosophy of life, which typifies that of so many others living in our Western spirit of pragmatism:

> Don't go to church on Sundays to pray to some unknown being who hasn't shown up in thousands of years to come and save you. You need to get off your knees, roll up your sleeves and save yourself.... How can Christianity address the problems of air pollution, nuclear proliferation and overpopulation when it is geared toward the issues of Jesus Christ's day: the domination of Rome and grinding slavery? Jesus tried to give his contemporaries hope in the next world, because he could see that there was no hope in the current one.[3]

Self-sufficiency is a myth that we believe in; the basis for all our strivings. Yet, we are beginning to reap only alienation and gnawing loneliness—the result of divinizing ourselves and forsaking God as the ultimate source of all power, gifts and talents we possess. Such illusory self-sufficiency inflates our pride until we live entirely in self-imposed isolation from God, other human beings and even the material world around us.

Need for humility

I have dared to write this book on humility, knowing full well that even Christians might automatically dismiss it, considering it a return to a long outmoded way of putting down our basic goodness. No doubt, the subject of humility has had a "bad press." I have outlined in the first two chapters some of the reasons for our disdain of traditional teachings on humility and our failure to incorporate humility into our daily lives.

In the following chapters I seek to highlight the nature of true humility, especially as found in the teaching of Jesus and his humble lifestyle on this earth, particularly in his public ministry.

God-Trinity is boundless love by nature, without any limitation that could lead to false pride. Only Christ and God's created beings—angels and us humans—can possess the virtue of humility. As human, Jesus had in fact limitations. He needed to grow in faith, hope and love of the Father. He humbled himself by emptying himself (Ph 2:7, 8), dying for love of us. He thus images the love within the Trinity, which pours out toward us in the uncreated energies of the Father, Son and Holy Spirit. Christ bridges God's perfect and constant love for us. In him we come to know that love and humility are distinct but inseparable.

Mary, the humble handmaid of the Lord who gave birth to the Son of God, is the archetype of what each of us must be like before God and neighbor. She is also the archetype of the Church, called to bring about the transfiguration of this universe into the total Christ.

Before such scriptural teaching and examples of authentic humility, how can we convert and become gentle and humble of heart? There is a great need to offset the humanistic psychology which claims that our human nature is "okay" in itself. Sin is too negative in such a view to be a focus of any human attention! Yet, we begin to acquire true humility when the Holy Spirit gives us greater self-knowledge and we confess our brokenness and sinfulness before the Lord, recognizing our need of a Savior. T. S. Eliot wrote: "The only wisdom we can hope to acquire is the wisdom of humility; humility is endless."[4]

The last four chapters deal with ways by which we can enter into developing true humility. Our living in a humble manner before God must be reflected in relationships of truth and justice. Authentic humility is a necessary therapy for overcoming false pride and sin in our members (Rm 7:24), in order to fulfill God's plan for us, who made us according to his image and likeness, Jesus Christ (Gn 1:26-27).

Death unto new life

The reality of death will always laugh at us, negating what we call life through its wall of darkness and nothingness. Only love that is humble dares to embrace death-dealing opportunities in our daily human situations, and above all in our final death. It hopes in the power of the humble Servant of Yahweh, who died freely out of love for us, but then was glorified and empowered by the Father to bring us new life through humility.

God-Trinity is always holding out to his chosen children the choice between life and death, between humility and pride, just as he offered it to his chosen people in the desert:

> I set before you life or death, blessing or curse. Choose life, then, so that you and your descendants may live in the love of Yahweh your God, obeying his voice, clinging to him; for in this your life consists, and on this depends your long stay in the land which Yahweh swore to your fathers Abraham, Isaac and Jacob he would give them. (Dt 30:19-20)

Negatively, humility is total self-emptying of all that impedes the fullness of divine life, the fusion of our spirit with God's Spirit. Positively, it is the life of our spirit, knowing, loving, possessing, and delighting in God, our neighbor, and all creation in the same divine light. In a word, one who loves knows nothing but love. To be truly empty and humble of heart is to receive riches from the only triune community of perfect love and "to act justly, to love tenderly and to walk humbly with your God" (Mi 6:8).

I pray that you who read this book and I who wrote it will allow the Holy Spirit of the gentle and humble Jesus to touch us deeply in our hearts. May we be wounded by the Trinity's love, indwelling at the core of our being, and passionately desire to journey inwardly to the abyss of our nothingness. And may we continually beg for the grace that God-Trinity may be the source, the center and the ultimate goal of our every thought, word and deed! Let us together learn of Jesus, gentle and humble of heart!

Whatever Happened to Humility?

We are entering in Western civilization into a period of tremendous inner emptiness and meaninglessness. We have become alienated from God, from the loved ones in our families, from other human beings, as well as from the natural world around us. We are a people who live habitually "disconnected" from a loving, intimate community; removed from the love of those who "love us into our true selves," without which we can never find our true identity.

We were made by God to live in harmony with him as our primary source of life and the goal of all our striving. Yet, TV and the printed word present to us an image of bland human beings, bored with life, seeking often by violence to find some way out of their boredom. The gross commercialism has presented us as insatiable consumers, absolutely needing the latest beauty aids, the newest dog and cat food. We appear to be a manipulated automaton ruled by good old Hal, who programs us to what we should desire and then sends us out to fulfill those desires.

The Austrian psychiatrist Victor E. Frankl has pointed out the growing *angst* or anxiety that fills the hearts of modern men and women with a sense of meaninglessness:

> Effectively an ever-increasing number of our clients today suffer from a feeling of interior emptiness—which I have described as existential emptiness—a feeling of total absence of a meaning to existence.[1]

You and I sit in the narrowness of our world, confused, yet somehow suspecting that we were made for something greater. Does not holy scripture call us noble creatures, made according to God's own image and likeness (Gn 1:26-27)? Is not our destiny to become participators of God's very own nature (2 P 1: 4)?

How beautiful and noble we are is described by the Psalmist:

> Ah, what is man that you should spare a thought for him; the son of man, that you should care for him? Yet you have made him little less than a god, you have crowned him with glory and splendor, made him lord over the work of your hands, set all things under his feet. (Ps 8:4-6)

Our true greatness

Our true greatness consists in being so loved by God that he has given to each of us his own Son, the Word enfleshed, "so that everyone who believes in him may not be lost, but may have eternal life" (Jn 3:16). Under the illumination of the Spirit of Jesus we are called to experience that we are really daughters and sons of a loving Father (Rm 8:15; Ga 4:6).

Jesus Christ is the image of the invisible God (Col 1:15) according to whom we have been created. We grow into our true, human greatness by responding to the call of Jesus to become one with him, a loving child of the heavenly Father. This necessitates our free decision to accept a healthy and noble submission in truth and justice to Jesus Christ, to become the unique person God is calling each of us to become in his Son Jesus.

The Protestant theologian Emil Brunner describes this awesome responsibility given to us human beings to respond freely to God's call:

> The necessity for decision, an obligation which he can never evade, is the distinguishing feature of man . . . it is

the being created by God to stand "over-against" him, who can reply to God, and who in this answer alone fulfills—or destroys—the purpose of God's creation.[2]

The true image of Jesus

Over the two thousand years of Christianity we have been given various images of who Jesus Christ is. There is the image of Jesus-Jew, Jesus-Pantocrator, Jesus-Caesar, Jesus-Monk, Jesus-Doctor, Jesus-Bridegroom, Jesus-Torquemada (of the Inquisition), Sweet Jesus, Jesus-Reformer, Jesus-Femina, Jesus-Gay and Jesus Christ Superstar.[3]

But the image that rings truest to the gospels is that of Jesus, humble of heart. This is the Jesus encountered by his first followers, and the one who most of us moderns desperately search for in our own lives. He asked all who wished to enter into the new creation of eternal life through an intimate union with him, that they should learn of him how to become humble of heart. Thus they would be able to love God with their whole heart and love others as they love themselves.

Whatever happened to true humility?

What is your immediate reaction when you hear the word *humility*? Don't you conjure up an image of a person with low self-esteem? Don't you picture a type of human being who is fawning, sycophant, a weakling and courting the favor of the powerful, according to the model of Dickens' Uriah Heep?

Webster's dictionary defines humility as: "A state or quality of being humble in spirit. Freedom from pride and arrogance." Perhaps many of us modern Christians have received a distorted view of humility in negative terms, expressed, for example, in that classic of medieval spirituality, *The Imitation of Christ* by Thomas à Kempis, who wrote:

You have nothing whereof you can glory, but many things for which you ought to account yourself vile; for you are much weaker than you are able to comprehend.[4]

A culture that opposes humility

Our modern Western culture has virtually ignored humility, considering it a denial of one's intrinsic worth as an individual. There has been much confusion in our understanding of pride and humility. Some psychologists have vigorously reacted to this by insisting on the necessity of a healthy pride and a good esteem of ourselves and our talents.

Webster's *New International Dictionary* defines pride as: "Inordinate self-esteem; an unrealistic conceit or superiority in talents, beauty, wealth, rank, etc." The psychologist Willard Gaylin presents a different view of pride:

> As a psychoanalyst in mid-twentieth-century America, I view pride as a virtue and its absence the deficiency of our time. The restoration of pride is a major goal in treatment. Self-respect and self-value are essential components which underlie the healthy (good) life.[5]

Pride versus humility

Should we have a more positive view of pride and humility? Dr. Robert J. Furey poses the question and leads us to a more balanced view of both:

> So who is right? Is pride healthy or unhealthy? The answer is that pride is a very positive characteristic which can easily become destructive. When feelings of pride turn destructive, however, they are properly called feelings of conceit, arrogance or superiority. Pride describes

a feeling of positive regard for ourselves, a very healthy feeling. . . . Without humility, pride becomes conceit and arrogance. . . . Without pride, humility becomes passivity and complacency. Together, pride and humility form a foundation for healthy growth. If we begin to pay more attention to humility, pride may one day become a virtue.[6]

Self-sufficiency

Our technological world tends to de-humanize individuals and reduce them to functional robots with no worth or self-esteem. This risks to undo the delicate balance between a true Christian pride, based on God's loving graces and our own free cooperation, and an authentic humility that allows us to accept our limitations and shortcomings. Accepting our frailties and sins, our weaknesses and evils, we might refuse to accept any responsibility for a personal change, for a repentance of sorrow for failing to be our true, noble self. By over-emphasizing our pride, instead, we might end in a self-imposed isolation from God and all human beings in an anti-societal *self-sufficiency*.

The theologian Samuel Dresner describes this most prevalent tendency in our modern society as:

> The sin of which modern man is most frequently found guilty is that of "self-sufficiency." It is the belief that man is sufficient unto himself and needs no divine authority and guide. It is the certainty that man is capable of fathoming all secrets, of controlling all events, of mastering all situations, even of achieving a utopian society of peace and prosperity which would endure until the end of time.[7]

Islands unto ourselves

With the aid of many humanistic psychologists we see a phenomenon growing in Western, affluent countries that refuses to allow God to be the center of all created reality. It substitutes the individual human ego as the center of all one's thoughts, desires and strivings. The result is very evident in our immense rate of divorces, the breakup of any self-sacrificing commitments to each other and to one's children, along with the growing hatred for certain minorities due to race, color or creed.

Such a spirit of selfishness might be the main reason why true humility is not very popular in today's society. Morality becomes very relative to our selfish whims, and there is no openness toward God's commandments. Children bring guns to school, kill their playmates and show no remorse. By society considering humility a negative trammeling to the individual creativity, we also see the continued erosion of any sense of sin among great numbers of human beings today.

Whatever became of sin?

In his book, *Whatever Became of Sin?* Dr. Karl Menninger insists that much of the problem of society's ills today lies in the ignoring of the reality of personal sin and responsible guilt, recognized and rectified by all of us. He writes:

> In all of the laments and reproaches made by our seers and prophets, one misses any mention of "sin," a word which used to be a veritable watchword of prophets. It was a word once in everyone's mind, but now rarely if ever heard. Does that mean that no sin is involved in all our troubles—sin with an "I" in the middle? Is no one any longer guilty of anything? Guilty perhaps of a sin that

could be repented and repaired or atoned for? Is it only that someone may be stupid or sick or criminal—or asleep? Wrong things are being done, we know; tares are being sown in the wheat field at night. But is no one responsible, no one answerable for these acts? Anxiety and depression we all acknowledge, and even vague guilt feelings; but has no one committed any sins?[8]

Lack of repentance and forgiveness

Our exalted sense of self-sufficiency truly leads to this lack of any sense of sin. We refuse to accept our guilt and to have remorse for having chosen death through our blatant pride, rather than life through true repentance. We neglect to reflect on the inner powers, especially those that lie within our unconscious, and which Paul describes as his "unspiritual self" that is "sin in his members" (Rm 8:24).

We are proud to be tolerant toward persons of different nationalities, color and religious beliefs. Yet, we fail to recognize how often we pass judgment on others, having little knowledge of their background and life-experiences. We are like Albert Camus' gin-sodden lawyer in his novel, *The Fall*. Both the lawyer and we live near the hellish canals of Amsterdam. We are the judge of everyone, but never the penitent. Proud persons see a humble, inner attention to control our thoughts and moods and to bring them under "dominion and captivity to Jesus Christ" (2 Co 10:5) as an inhibition against personal freedom and creativity.

The words of the sixth-century desert Father Dorotheos still apply to most of us:

> Every one of us is very careful, on every occasion, to throw the blame on his brother and to strike him down with its weight. Every one of us is negligent and keeps

none of the commandments, and we demand in return that our neighbors keep them all.[9]

This attitude can only be overcome by true humility, which necessitates a vital relationship to a personal God, the source of truth and justice. Such a relativistic morality, which is no true morality, has been strongly condemned by Pope John Paul II in his encyclical, *Veritatis Splendor*:

> According to some, it appears that one no longer need acknowledge the enduring absoluteness of any moral value. All around us we encounter contempt for human life after conception and before birth; the ongoing violation of basic rights of the person; the unjust destruction of goods minimally necessary for a human life.[10]

Does humility mean subservience?

Another reason why the modern world rejects the concept of humility is that for many of us it has for centuries connoted a spirit of subservience toward the authority figures in our society. Is it not true that humility has been a buzz word from time immemorial for women and whole classes of societies to consider themselves inferior to others? Today many individuals and groups move to throw off the shackles of prejudices against them that held them in low self-esteem.

How many women have been told by their pastors that their husbands would not abuse them if they were more docile and obedient to them as the true head of the household? Women in their homes were taught that their task was to give continued, "unselfish" sacrifice. We also think of the terrifying caste systems imposed on certain groups of people, who were encouraged in a spirit of fatalism to humbly accept to do their *karma* to be eventually "liberated." We think of the black slave, man and woman, who in America was taught socially and religiously to be humble and debased before the master-owner.

Humility defined by theologians

A great factor that has diminished any enthusiasm for the development of humility in our modern times was the traditional approaches and definitions of humility by theologians and spiritual writers of the Middle Ages. In the twelfth century, Bernard defined humility as "a virtue by which a person, knowing himself as he truly is, abases himself."[11]

Thomas Aquinas defined humility similarly: "Humility is the virtue by which a person considers his weak nature and places himself in the lowest position according to his own situation." [12] In another definition he also stresses not striving for higher things and to be submissive to those in higher authority. "The virtue of humility consists in keeping oneself within one's own bounds, not reaching out to things above oneself, but to submit to one's superior."[13]

Using Aristotle's treatment of human virtues, Thomas and his successors spilt much ink on distinguishing the uniqueness of humility and whether it is related to the virtues of magnanimity and temperance—a real yawner for most modern persons.

Spiritual formation

Laypersons, religious men and women, as well as priests and ministers, were all too often instructed by their spiritual directors to consider humility in negative terms, opposing the deadly sin of all sins, pride. If pride is an exaggerated opinion of oneself, denying at least implicitly that God alone is the source of all good, then humility, in turn, teaches to consider oneself as of no decent account, always prone toward sin based on pride.

Would you agree with me that we are not enthusiastic to develop humility in our spiritual life, because our Christian teachers and preachers linked humility with repressing a healthy pride, a God-given self-respect and a longing to be esteemed by others?

Abraham Maslow describes this "good" self-esteem as a sign of the psychologically healthy person. We all have a need for a non-exaggerated but firmly based positive evaluation of ourselves. "All peoples reported in literature seemed to have pride, to prefer to be liked, to seek respect and status, to avoid anxiety."[14]

Pragmatism and human dignity

One obstacle for living in a true balance between a proper self-esteem and a humble stance before God, neighbor and the entire created world comes from our Western, technological culture. This society dictates to us that our worth lies in the quantity of our possessions, especially money, the symbol of "power," which enables us to buy expensive playthings like million-dollar mansions, yachts, costly cars and wardrobes.

We are reckoned in the obituary columns as famous or important, as one who has lived a full and "creative" life, by what important things we accomplished while on this earth and with what important friends we associated. Our society forces us to find our uniqueness in competitiveness toward others. When persons retire in our country, they are often considered to have come to a stop, not only in their produc-tivity, but also in their value to society.

An essential element of true humility is the realization that we are not God but human. Therefore, by our very nature we will always be limited in our gifts and abilities. It is very human to honestly accept our limitations, our failures and mistakes, and above all our deliberate sinfulness before a God who has no limitations but has become one with us in his only begotten Son, Jesus Christ. But Christ, being from all eternity in equality with God, "emptied himself to assume the condition of a slave, and became as human beings are; and being as all human beings are, he was humbler yet, even to accepting death, death on a cross" (Ph 2:7-8).

Perhaps the ultimate answer to "Whatever happened to humility?" must be that we Christians know and understand the incredibly good news that we have been destined by God to become his children in and through Christ. This understanding is possible through the revelation that Jesus became limited and was tempted in all things but did not sin (Heb 4:15). Yet, we continue to disbelieve his revelation and his intimate indwelling presence, one with the Father and the Holy Spirit. Thus we continue to live in the lies of our all-consuming pride and fail to balance our inner dignity with the need to be ever vigilant over every thought, word and deed, since there is sin within us and all around us.

Walk with integrity and humility with God

Jesus is saying to us, his disciples: "Here I am; this place is holy. Here you are to learn of me and become humble as I am. So take off your shoes, your self-reliance, throw your fig-leaf securities to the wind and approach this burning bush to become consumed by the fire of my divine love for you." This is the highest union, the infused union with Christ and through him with the Trinity, in which God communicates himself as Father, Son and Spirit. It can never be achieved by conceptual knowledge, but only by an immediate, experiential knowledge, wherein he opens himself to us if we ardently desire to receive such a grace. True humility is the gift of the

Holy Spirit given to the "little ones," the ones who, like Jesus, in the words of Bernanos, present to God "the wonder of empty hands."

Acquiring humility lies not so much in what we do but in the gift that awaits us when we open the door of our heart, and we stand before him who has always been there. He reveals that his infinite love for us, which is one with that of the Trinity, is also a self-emptying love in which humility and love become one. And we ache in the depths of our being to become more truthful and beautiful, to die to everything that is a lie, deceit, or false pride, and to find a true pride, one with true humility. We become humbler still in amazement, as we experience the perfect love and infinite mercy of God in Christ Jesus, who reveals how much more God's love would still want to make of us, and what instead we have been in our wandering "lostness" to Love itself.

Perhaps now we are ready to examine the characteristics of what *true humility* means.

The Nature of True Humility

Would we consider ourselves to be truly humble persons? Our first reaction to such a question would probably be that we really have not given humility much consideration amidst so many other more pressing matters. We have seen some of the reasons why we turn away from the topic of humility. We thus, in general, entertain little or no enthusiasm to read and meditate on this virtue, which traditionally has been considered as a most essential one, and which Jesus has strongly commanded us to learn from his humble life as found in the gospels.

Realistically, when was the last time you heard a sermon on the necessity of humility as the foundation of all other moral virtues, and of the relationships between you and God, between you, your neighbor and the entire created world?

In preparing to write this book I checked the card catalog in a Catholic university that offers a master's degree in theology and Christian spirituality. To my surprise I found not one book devoted to humility. The librarian told me that there may have been books on humility, but that they were probably donated to seminary libraries in Africa, since the topic would not be too relevant for the twentieth century!

In a word, should we not admit that we are simply not interested in the subject of humility? The main reason is, perhaps, that for a long time we have entertained distorted ideas about humility and have not understood its *real* nature. Thus we have not understood the great need for humility in our relationships with God and neighbor at home, at work, in our parishes and toward our church leaders.

25

Knowledge beyond reason

John Climacus of the seventh century cautions us in searching for the nature of humility. We are to avoid any exclusively rational explanation of what humility truly means. This treasure is of a quality that eludes adequate description:

> It carries an inscription of heavenly origin which is therefore incomprehensible, so that anyone seeking words for it is faced with a great and endless task. The inscription on this treasure reads as follows: "Holy Humility."[1]

Climacus goes on to develop the importance of investigating the topic of humility with a reverence and a docile receptivity to God's grace, since it is a gift he gives to the lowly:

> Humility is a grace in the soul and with a name known only to those who have had experience of it. It is indescribable wealth, a name and a gift from God.
>
> "Learn from me," Jesus said; that is, not from an angel, not from a human person, not from a book, but "from me," that is, from my dwelling within you, from my illumination and action within you, for "I am gentle and meek of heart" (Mt 11:29) in thought and in spirit, and your souls will find rest from conflicts and relief from evil thoughts.[2]

Still, we can learn much about the nature of true humility by examining first the etymology of the root concept of the word itself, then its meaning in scripture, and finally the various explanations by theologians and spiritual writers in the Christian tradition.

Earthy humility

The term itself is derived from the Latin word, *humus*, which means the earth or the soil. It refers to our earthly origin from lowly matter. From earthy matter we came forth and into the material earth we will again return. When we apply this term to any person or thing, the word has the connotation of something or someone who is abject, ignoble or a thing that is of poor condition and, therefore, of no great value.

When it is used strictly for a person, humility refers to the afflictions and miseries which may happen to an individual from some outside agents, as for example when someone humiliates a person by afflicting sufferings upon the other.

In a more ethical sense humility could refer to the modest esteem individuals might have for themselves, shown by a humble attitude of submission toward others. The dominant stress in the Greek, classical sense of humility, *tapeinos*, is on our human creaturehood, as given to us by God. Thus we did not always exist as necessary without a beginning and end, like the supreme source of all being, God.[3]

Humility in the Old Testament

From the very first pages in the Book of Genesis, Yahweh is presented as the gratuitous Creator of all the material world of created beings. Nothing of matter has eternal, independent existence, but is willed into being by God's continued and conserving command: "Let there be. . ." But after the entire sub-human cosmos has come into being, God as a We-community changes from the imperative, "Let there be. . . " to the indicative: "Let us make man in our image, after our likeness. . . . And so God created man in his own image, in the image of God he created him; male and female he created them" (Gn 1:26-27).

Yahweh freely chooses the Israelites as his elected people and promises to protect them against their enemies, as he will always be faithful to the covenant he has made with them, if they will humbly obey his statutes and commands.

Humility and obedient submission is seen as the fitting relation on the part of his people, who should always do God's will and never forget that they are God's sheer gifts, "emptied receptacles to be filled with God's goodness," in the words of Irenaeus of the second century.

The Book of Job summarizes this attitude of God's chosen people toward their Creator: "When men are cast down, then you will say,'There is a lifting up; and he shall save the humble person' " (Jb 22:29). The psalms abound with God's promise to lift up the humble:

> The meek will he guide in judgment; and the meek will he teach his way. (Ps 25:9)
> For the Lord takes pleasure in his people; he will beautify the meek with salvation. (Ps 149:4)

In the sapiential literature of the Old Testament we see humility and lowliness of spirit as a sign of wisdom before God:

> When pride comes, then there comes shame; but with the lowly is wisdom. (Pr 11:2)
> The fear of the Lord is the instruction of wisdom; and before honor is humility. (Pr 15:33)
> By humility and the fear of the Lord are riches, and honor and life. (Pr 22:4)
> Let rich and noble and poor take pride in fearing the Lord. (Si 10:25)

Humility in the New Testament

The fundamental teaching that Jesus and his disciples re-
peat to us over and over is that to receive the kingdom of God
we need to convert and become humble like children.

> Father, Lord of heaven and earth! I thank you because
> you have shown to the unlearned what you have hidden
> from the wise and learned. Yes, Father, this was how you
> were pleased to have it happen. (Lk 10:21)
> I assure you that unless you change and become like
> children, you will never enter the kingdom of heaven.
> The greatest in the kingdom of heaven is the one who
> humbles himself and becomes like this child. (Mt 18:3-4)

Thus we see a different sign of greatness in God's kingdom.
God exalts the lowly (Lk 1:52). "If one of you wants to be great,
he must be the servant of the rest; and if one of you wants to
be first, he must be your slave, like the Son of man, who did
not come to be served but to serve and to give his life to redeem
many people" (Mt 20:26-28).

God will consider as truly justified only the humble who
are aware of their nothingness before him because of their
personal sinfulness. This is what Jesus taught us in his parable
of the Pharisee and the publican. He concludes this parable,
again stressing the importance of humility to receive forgiveness of sins: "For everyone who makes himself great will be
humbled, and everyone who humbles himself will be made
great" (Lk 18:14).

A humble servant

Jesus brings about a revolution in the concept of humility
that was not even stressed in the Old Testament. It is only

because he himself, eternally one with the Father (Ph 2:6), did not hold on to his dignity as truly divine by nature, but "emptied himself," becoming even more humble by being obedient unto death, death on the cross. He came to become humble love by becoming the suffering servant of Yahweh (Is 52-53), serving each of us by suffering on our behalf so that we might share in his divine life through grace.

In his gospel John presents us with the powerful, symbolic action of Jesus washing the feet of his disciples. This symbolic act is a summary not only of the way Jesus lived in loving service for the poor and broken ones, but also of the way the Trinity lives in self-emptying love for us.

> I, your Lord and Teacher, have just washed your feet. You, then, should wash one another's feet. I have set an example for you, so that you will do just what I have done for you. (Jn 13:14-15)

Teachings of theologians and writers

In the Christian tradition we find a continued and long line of theologians and spiritual writers, who present us with a unified analysis of the nature of authentic Christian humility. Reflecting on holy scripture and especially on Jesus' New Testament teachings and his humble lifestyle, these thinkers agree that charity is the culmination of all perfection, without which nothing else has any value (1 Co 13:1-13). But they are also unanimous in teaching that humility and self-denial are the foundation of perfection and the condition of any real progress.[4]

John Cassian of the fourth century brings the teachings of the Fathers and Mothers of the desert into Western spirituality, especially into the monasticism of Benedict. He writes in his *Institutes*: "It is plain to see, then, that no advance in perfection and purity of life can be made except through real humility, which is to be shown first towards the brethren and also to God in the depths of the heart."[5]

Gregory the Great writes:

> Since humility is the very source of virtue, it follows that a virtue will spring up and endure if it is rooted in humility, but if it is cut off from this root, it will wither away because it lacks the life-giving sap of charity.[6]

In his Twelve Degrees of Humility, Bernard defines humility as "the virtue by which a person recognizes his own unworthiness because he really knows himself."[7] Thomas Aquinas brought his systematic thinking to an acute analysis of the nature of humility in opposition to pride, the source of all moral evil. Using categories from Aristotelian philosophy, Thomas defines humility both negatively and positively and demonstrates its unique importance as a "moderating" foundation for all other virtues.

> Humility restrains the appetite from aiming at great things against right reason; while magnanimity urges the mind to great things in accord with right reason. Hence it is clear that magnanimity is not opposed to humility: indeed they concur in this that each is according to right reason.[8]

Humility is placed in the power of our human will as are all virtues. There can be no true humility, according to Thomas, without true self-knowledge, which necessitates that we do not regard ourselves to be more than what we are before God.[9] Our will holds in restrain any exalting of ourselves above our objective gifts—gifts understood as given to our nothingness by God for his greater glory. What seems to be a negative self-abasement can be seen positively as a true manifestation of our metaphysical relationship with God, the source of all being. "Hence the fact that humility is caused by reverence for God does not prevent it from being a part of modesty or temperance."[10]

A needed distinction

So much of our modern misunderstanding and lack of appreciation of humility comes, I believe, from our reading of theologians and even the great saints of the Church who have written on the nature of humility. A distinction is needed. First, we see that humility is necessary in order to avoid the sin of pride that is the root of all sins. This is what Thomas is concerned with, as he presents humility as the antithesis of pride, which is the seeking or loving inordinately one's own excellence.[11]

The other approach to humility we see especially in the writings of the great saints, who aggressively sought to overcome pride by despising themselves in the light of their creatureliness and their past sins.[12]

I am the greatest sinner

This is the logical place to briefly consider the oft-repeated statement of many great saints, who were convinced that of all human beings they were the greatest of sinners.

How could they respect and prefer others, even those who possessed lesser spiritual gifts, without doing an injustice to God, who poured out so many natural and supernatural gifts onto these great athletes of the spiritual life?

Humility, as charity, focuses upon our double relationship with God and neighbor. As regards our relationship with God, we consider humility as the virtue that acknowledges him as the supreme giver of all gifts, even the gift of our own created being. We can thus honestly affirm that we are nothing outside of God's uncreated energies of divine love.

Regarding the relationship with our neighbors, humility does not require us to esteem our God-given gifts and graces less than similar ones found in others. As Paul directs us, "We have received the Spirit sent by God, so that we may know all that God has given us" (1 Co 2:12). There is a God-given, inner tendency to rightly esteem ourselves as the recipients of God's participated perfections, as we strive to become unique persons by God's grace. There is room for true self-esteem. But does it contradict the advice of the saints to despise ourselves? It does not when we see both true self-esteem and the desire to despise ourselves as the least of all human beings from different points of view.

On the one hand, God gives us our personal dignity to reflect somehow, even though in a limited way, his infinite beauty and perfection. He does this by the gratuitous bestowal of gifts upon us, especially in wishing to make us according to his own image and likeness (Gn 1:26). On the other hand, this desire for self-esteem, recognized not only by ourselves but also by others, must be controlled because of the sinful tendency into which we are all born, namely, to be "biased toward self" without any reference to God the giver of all good and beauty.

Paul enjoins upon us Christians:

> Do not do anything from selfish ambition or from a cheap desire to boast, but be humble toward one another, always considering others better than yourselves. (Ph 2:3)

Preferring others to ourselves

We begin to touch the core of true humility, as we seek to reconcile a proper love of self, of God's gifts and of his merciful forgiveness of our sins, with a proper love of others, to the point of esteeming them better than ourselves. We look at our personal sins and realize how much evil we could still do, if we would not walk humbly before the Lord and rejoice in his forgiving love. With this understanding of our personal esteem before God we can gladly accept slights, humiliations and even contempt and insults from others with an inner peace and joy. The basis for this is the conviction of Francis of Assisi: "I am only what I am before the Lord." Jesus Christ must increase, and we can honestly desire to decrease, as John the Baptist did (Jn 3:30).

The Fathers of the Church are unanimous in their teaching of how we can, in Paul's words, "be humble toward one another, always considering others better than ourselves" (Ph 2:3). We can esteem the potentially good, either hidden or evident energies in others that perhaps we ourselves do not possess. To keep the balance of true respect for others and proper esteem for ourselves, we need to call on the Lord to increase our humility. Esteeming our neighbors' hidden or manifested gifts, and considering our own sins and failings of which others are not as aware as we are, can help us in this. Each of us is unique in our sins, temptations and failures and the depth of evil we are capable of. No one else knows this as well as we do, not even the neighbor we are confronting and below whom we are humbly placing ourselves.

Summary of the nature of humility

Humility, therefore, is the direct opposite of any pride. Pride builds in us a desire of absolute or relative power, leading us to focus upon our false or unspiritual self, by forgetting that separated from God we don't "count for much." An abiding awareness of the supremacy of God is the main reference for all the good and beauty we possess. Thus we can say that the fullness of humility can only be found in a personal, faithful encounter with God.

We therefore find three necessary elements constituting true Christian humility.[13] The first is that we become more and more aware of God as the supreme Creator, and that we human beings owe our very existence and all the gifts we possess to God. This shows humility not to be the greatest of all virtues, since it requires our awareness of this truth. It is not a purely supernatural gift like faith, hope and love, which are given to us as the foundation of all other virtues.[14]

Humility is based on the *truth* of God's necessary existence as the supreme source of all other created beings, and on *justice*, which seeks to move our will to be aware of God at the center of all our striving and to render glory and praise to him in all our thoughts, words and deeds.

The second element of authentic humility flows from the sense of God's holiness, goodness and beauty, in all his transcendence and majesty. As we become aware of God in what Rudolph Otto calls, "the *mysterium tremendum*,"[15] we also become aware of our brokenness and sinfulness. We not only understand by God's grace how we completely depend upon him and are justly always in his debt, but we realize affectively in our heart the heinousness of our sins and how ungrateful and arrogant we have been, having turned away from God's perfect love. This becomes therapeutic healing if it is grounded in the beauty and glorious goodness of God, who prevents us from falling into despair and opens us up to an ardent return of love and joy.

Our awareness of the glory of God develops in us a childlike and joyful abandonment to live only for God. Francis of Assisi's realization becomes our own as we confront the allness of God and our own weakness and sinfulness: "My God and my all!" Humility positively fills us with a liberating spirit of reverence toward God that brings us inner joy and a new-found sense of our uniqueness in God to whom we constantly seek to render honor and glory, as James writes:

It is all that is good, everything that is perfect, which is given us from above; it comes down from the Father of all light. (Ja 1:16-17)

Remembering God's goodness

The third element of true humility is to remember in our brokenness and sinfulness the supreme goodness of God's eternal plan and his constant fidelity to bring our salvation about with our humble cooperation. We ground our humility on God's free choice to make us human beings according to his own image and likeness (Gn 1:26-27).

True humility allows us to recognize our radical predestination to become participators of God's very own nature (2 P 1:4). With the psalmist we can be aware of our inner beauty to reflect as an individual something of God's perfect beauty.

Yet you have made him little less than a god, you have crowned him with glory and splendor, made him lord over the work of your hands, set all things under his feet. (Ps 8:5-6)

The more we receive of God's goodness and respond according to our dignity as a loving child of so loving a Father in Jesus through their Holy Spirit, the more we abandon ourselves to God in each moment, as we trust in him to be our strength when we are weakest. Such childlike faith and trust are therefore graceful gifts of God's personal love for us, the broken, little ones in his kingdom.

Complete abandonment is our true response to his fidelity. How beautifully Paul describes this self-surrender to God through the humble self-sacrifice of Jesus Christ for love of us:

If God is for us, who can be against us? Certainly not God, who did not even keep back his own Son, but offered him for us all! He gave us his Son—will he not also freely give us all things? Who will accuse God's chosen people? . . . Not Christ Jesus, who died, or rather, who was raised to life and is at the right side of God, pleading with him for us! . . . There is nothing in all creation that will ever be able to separate us from the love of God, which is ours through Christ Jesus our Lord. (Rm 8:31-39)

The basis for Christian humility: Jesus Christ

We have pointed out that God-Trinity could never possess the human virtue of humility, since God is perfect love without any limitations, without any temptation to be proud. To desire something other than what the Trinity is by its essence would be a contradiction within the Trinity. God is the fullness of being and therefore could never desire to be made more than he always is.

But in order to communicate God's perfect love for us, Jesus Christ, God-man, has freely consented to taking upon himself our humanity, with all its inherited limitations, even to the point of submitting himself to be tempted in all things, save sin (Heb 4:15). He emptied himself in his great love for us unto his death on the cross (Ph 2:7-8). Jesus is incarnate humility. There never was, nor ever will be, a greater humility than that of Christ.

He alone is the greatest bridge-builder, the *Pontifex Maximus*, who is at the same time perfect love as God and perfect humility as man. He unites the greatest virtue of charity with humility, so that by the Holy Spirit's infusion of faith, hope and love into us, we now can not only realize love and humility intellectually but also live it in our hearts. In Jesus these two were never separated, and as we learn from him how to be humble, we too will discover that there can be no true love without humility and no true humility without love.

Augustine gives a fitting summary of the importance of humility without which there can be no salvation, no holiness, no true love of God and neighbor. He writes:

> The sure road that leads to God is first humility, next humility and lastly humility. Ask me the question as often as you may, my answer will ever be the same. There are other precepts in God's law, but unless humility precede and follow our good works and also accompany them . . . unless we hold fast to it and repress pride and all vain self-conceit, our good deeds will be snatched out of our hands. . . . Pride lurks even in our good actions and must be guarded against lest it rob us of our merit.[16]

The Spirituality of the Anawim of God

In his classic, *Poverty of Spirit,* Johannes Metz well describes this scriptural attitude of us human beings toward God and neighbor: "Only through poverty of spirit do we draw close to God; only through it does God draw near to us. Poverty of spirit is the meeting place of heaven and earth, the mysterious place where God and we encounter each other, the point where infinite mystery meets concrete existence."[1]

God-Trinity has called us from all eternity to share the kingdom of God within the innermost sanctuary of our heart, the core of our being, where we possess the three divine persons. There we share in God's love, joy, peace, rest, and fruitfulness. Jesus promised us a kingdom of God which comes only to those who are poor in spirit.

For God's chosen children, poverty of spirit is the most basic and fundamental disposition of mind and heart. It is the experience in childlike trust of the love of their heavenly Father in and through the Son and the Holy Spirit. We who strive daily to become poor in spirit find our ancestors both in the Old and New Testament *anawim*: "the poor in spirit," "the little ones," "the lowly," "the humble of heart," "the handmaids" and "servants of the Lord." These, in their total childlike trust of God, place themselves completely at his disposal, so he can work in them all that he calls them to be as daughters and sons of his Son (Jn 1:12-13), participators of God's very own divine nature (2 Pt 1: 4). By this inner poverty and authentic humility before God and others, we respond to God's call to be holy as he is holy (Mt 5:48); merciful in all relations with our neighbors, as the Father is merciful to all his children (Lk 6:36); loving everyone as Christ loves us (Jn 15:12).

Meaning of anawim

The word, *anawim*, is plural for the Hebrew word, *anaw*, which originally meant "to be stooped, bowed, lowered, overwhelmed," as Father Gelin points out in his book, *The Poor of Yahweh*. From scripture, *anawim* took on a profound significance, essentially embodying the meaning of spirituality as found in both Testaments. Basically, *anawim* are persons poor in spirit, the lowly and humble of heart, the true handmaids and servants of the Lord, who place their entire trust in God. This is epitomized in the saying of Jesus:

> The kingdom of God belongs to those who have hearts as trusting as these little children. And anyone who does not have their kind of faith will never get within the kingdom's gates. Truly I say to you, whoever does not receive the kingdom of God like a child will not enter it. (Lk 18:16-17)

The anawim in the Old Testament

"For Yahweh loves his people and he adorns the lowly [the *anawim*] with victory" (Ps 149:4). Throughout the Old Testament we find that the *anawim* are God's people—the ones he has prepared for himself (Is 60:21; 62:12; 63:8); the people who are faithful to his eternal covenant with them (Is 61:8); the real Israel, a blessed race (Is 65:9, 23); a holy people (Is 62:12); the authentic "elect" of God (Is 65:9, 15, 22); the redeemed (Is 62:12).

They are God's servants and handmaids (Is 44:1; 54:17), his disciples (Is 54:13) who keep the law imprinted upon their hearts (Is 51:7). The *anawim* place all their hope in the Lord (Ps 50:9). They find their refuge in him (Ps 33:9). They are the little ones, the poor and humble of heart. "May the humble not retire in confusion, may the poor and the afflicted [the *anawim*] praise your Name, O Lord" (Ps 73:21). "Yahweh hears the poor [the *anawim*], and his own who are in bonds he spurns not" (Ps 68:34).

The anawim in the teachings of the prophets

"Give praise, O you heavens and rejoice, O earth; you mountains, give praise with jubilation; because Yahweh has comforted his people and has shown mercy to his poor ones" (Is 49:13). It is mainly the great prophet Isaiah who expounds the doctrine about the *anawim* as God's favorite children. Over and over he writes that the poor, the little ones, the meek and humble of heart receive God's constant help and protection.

> He has sent me to preach to the meek [*anawim*], to heal the contrite of heart, and to preach a release to the captives and deliverance to them that are shut up, to proclaim the acceptable year of Yahweh, and the day of vengeance of our God, to comfort all that mourn. (Is 61:1-2)
>
> For thus says the High and Eminent that inhabits eternity: "I live in that high and holy place where those with a contrite and humble spirit live." (Is 57:17)
>
> [For] whom shall I have respect but him that is poor and little and of a contrite heart, and that trembles at my words. (Is 66:1-2)

In the Book of Psalms we find: "The Lord is close to those whose hearts are breaking and saves those who are of a contrite spirit" (34:18). If we are to imitate the *anawim* of the Old Testament, we must show total openness to God at all times, absolute humility, respect, obedience to his will, a conscious abiding spirit of compunction and repentance, a willingness to be used by God, and total trust in his promise to be faithful to his covenant, which binds him to his chosen people in total self-giving.

The prophets Amos, Isaiah, Jeremiah, Ezekiel, and other prophets of God reveal on the pages of scripture that God's promises, which were once entrusted to the people of Israel as a whole, would one day belong only to a small and select group of Israelites called the "Remnant," formed by God himself in preparation for the coming of the Messiah and the full establishment of the kingdom of God on this earth.

It is these Remnant, the poor of Yahweh (Is 49:13), who constitute the faithful, humble ones of Israel. They completely surrender themselves in obedience to God's commands out of total trust in his power. "For Yahweh loves his people and he adorns the lowly with the victory" (Ps 149:4). One day, all that the *anawim* of the Old Testament represent will be concentrated in Mary, the true link connecting the Old Testament with the New. She will be the consummation of the spirituality of the *anawim*, drawing into herself all the power of their welcome for the God who comes. She will epitomize the measureless longing that is the spiritual dimension of Israel, and which will at last bring forth Christ in the ineffable victory of the incarnation.

The anawim in the psalms

As we know, Jesus himself and his followers made the psalter their own most fruitful prayer to the Father as a summary of *anawim* spirituality. As we pray the psalms, in and with Jesus and through his Spirit, the author of the psalms, we cannot help but grow in the spirituality they express and beget in our hearts, that of the little ones who place all their trust in God. There is no characteristic of this spirituality of the poor in spirit that is not, in some divinely efficacious way, expressed for us in the psalms.

In psalm 34 we experience how the poor cry out to Yahweh: "A cry goes up from the poor man, and Yahweh hears and helps him in all his troubles" (v. 6). "Those who fear the Lord want for nothing" (v. 9). "The eyes of the Lord are turned toward the virtuous, his ears to their cry" (v. 15).

In psalm 51 the *anawim* weep for their sins and cry out unceasingly with the repentant David for mercy (v. 1, *passim*). "God, create a clean heart in me, put into me a new and constant spirit" (v. 10). "My sacrifice is this broken spirit, you will not scorn this crushed and broken heart" (v. 17).

The psalms are God's disclosure to his chosen people, the poor ones. They are his divine providence, his goodness and eternal mercy that is above all his works. Not only do the *anawim* accept such revelation as true, they thirst to respond to God's humble love toward them. They trust and show complete confidence in God's caring love, especially in times of trials and tribulations.

> Yahweh is my shepherd, I lack nothing. He guides me by paths of virtue for the sake of his name. Though I pass through a gloomy valley, I fear no harm; beside me your rod and your staff are there to hearten me. (Ps 23)

The anawim of God in the New Testament

How dramatically the New Testament portrays the *anawim*: "God chose what is foolish in the world to shame the wise; God chose what is weak in the world to confound the strong. God chose what is low and despised in the world, even things that are not, to bring to nothing things that are, so that no human being might boast in the presence of God" (1 Co 1:27-29).

As we have already stated, Mary is the true link connecting the Old and the New Covenant of God with us human beings.

It was in Nazareth that the announcement of the Messiah's coming was made to Mary, the new Eve. Her life reflected that of the desert *anawim*, the faithful ones who lived in inner desert silence, in total surrender in their emptiness to God's allness. Mary is the first of the New Testament *anawim* to be part of the Remnant of God. "Behold, I am the handmaid, the servant of the Lord; let it be done to me according to your word" (Lk 1:38).

She was totally at the disposition of God, the center of her life. Because of her humility and emptiness, he could do whatever he wished, even to incarnate Love itself, his only begotten Son. "Blessed are you, Mary, because you have believed that God would do all that he said" (Lk 1:45), is the homage paid to Mary by Elizabeth, her cousin. Mary's humble response is her Magnificat, which is the canticle of the *anawim* of the New Testament. In this beautiful heart-song we find distilled in lyrical language the perfect and living expression of the spirituality of the *anawim* of the desert.

> My soul magnifies the Lord and my spirit rejoices in God my Savior, because he has regarded the lowliness of his handmaid; for behold, henceforth all generations shall call be blessed; because he who is mighty has done great things to me, and holy is his name. (Lk 1:46-49)

Deeply conscious of her littleness, her radical poverty of spirit as a created being and handmaid of the Lord, Mary's heart breaks forth in an ecstasy of happiness and gratitude, knowing that in some hidden way she was at the very heart of the history of salvation. All ages to come will remember her and all ages past have prepared for this ineffable mystery of the incarnation. Only the truly humble can speak of their humility. "God chooses the weak things of this world" (1 Co 1:27).

Jesus: summit of anawim spirituality

On every page of the gospels we contemplate the great depths of Jesus' poverty of spirit, his total humility and limitless trust in his heavenly Father. We see him fulfilling the mission his Father gave him to bring about our redemption and divinization as sharers with him of divine life in the kingdom of God. In human form, especially as the poorest of the poor on the cross, he manifests the *anawim* community of the Trinity—persons who empty themselves in a gift of self-sacrificing love to each other. Thus they discover that emptiness is fullness, death is resurrection, to lose one's life in love for another is to really gain it.

For this reason Jesus calls us: "Come to me, all you who labor and are heavy laden, and I will give you rest. Take my yoke upon you, and learn from me; for I am gentle and lowly in heart, and you will find rest for your souls; for my yoke is easy and my burden light" (Mt 11:29). Our Lord does not merely say that he has all the spiritual qualities of the *anawim* but that he *is*, in his very being as the eternal Son and image of God, all these qualities. Jesus himself constitutes the very essence of the spirituality of the *anawim*, the very reality itself of radical poverty of spirit, humility of heart, complete trust in and abandonment to the heavenly Father.

Our oneness with the risen Lord

Because Jesus emptied himself totally for love of us, the Father raised him up in glory, and as we share even now through his Spirit in that glory, we are also able to identify with his radical poverty. As we put on the mind of Christ and by his Spirit live in love, we hunger also to be more emptied, made *nada*, as John of the Cross puts it. We desire deep prayerful union with Jesus, poor yet perfect image of the kenotic, emptying love of the Father and the Holy Spirit.

Negatively, poverty of spirit is total self-emptying of all that impedes the fullness of divine life, the fusion of our spirit with God's Spirit. Positively, it is the life of our spirit, knowing, loving, possessing, and delighting in God, our neighbor, and all creation in the same divine light. In a word, one who loves knows nothing but love. To be truly empty and poor of spirit is to receive riches from the only triune community of perfect love.

Jesus' Teaching on Humility

We have seen in previous chapters how Jesus lived on this earth humbly before the *allness* of the heavenly Father, both in his hidden and public life. Now we need to look at Jesus' teaching on humility as recorded in the gospels. "The word of God is alive and active, sharper than any double-edged sword. It cuts all the way through, to where soul and spirit meet, to where joints and marrow come together. It judges the desires and thoughts of the human heart. There is nothing that can be hidden from God; everything in all creation is exposed and lies open before his eyes. And it is to him that we must all give an account of ourselves" (Heb 4:12-13).

If Jesus came on this earth to be "the Way, the Truth and the Life" (Jn 14:6), then his teachings are life-giving. We need to examine Jesus' teachings on humility as recorded in the gospels. And we need to embrace what to our sin-laden minds, so clouded by self-centered pride, would appear as "folly" and a stumbling block, as it was to the Jews and the Gentiles and to most modern Christians today.

1. The Beatitudes (Matthew 5:1-12)

In Matthew's Sermon on the Mount, Jesus explains how those who accepted his preaching would possess the kingdom of God. He is the one who speaks in the place of God; the law Moses brought down from Mount Sinai and imposed upon his people is no longer. "It was said by God ... but *I* say to you. ... "

Let us ponder on what he teaches about the necessity of humility and meekness, if we are to enter into the kingdom of God.

Happy are those who know they are spiritually poor; the kingdom of heaven belongs to them! (Mt 5:3)

Happy are those who are humble; they will receive what God has promised! (5:5)

Happy are those who are merciful to others; God will be merciful to them! (5:7)

Happy are the pure in heart; they will see God! (5:8)

Happy are those who work for peace; God will call them his children! (5:9)

Happy are those who are persecuted because they do what God requires; the kingdom of heaven belongs to them! (5:10)

Happy are you when people insult you and persecute you and tell all kinds of evil lies against you because you are my followers. Be happy and glad, for a great reward is kept for you in heaven. (5:11-12)

In various ways Jesus describes the necessity of humility in order to enter intimately into relationship with the Trinity, "the kingdom of God," where God is all in the lives of Jesus' disciples. We see humility as the essential door through which we enter into God's kingdom. The blessings of both heaven and earth are received from God by the lowly in spirit. God blesses abundantly the poor in spirit. Such persons are not seen as possessing any special greatness in the eyes of the worldly ones, but God is greatly drawn to them in their ordinary, constant self-abandonment.

It is a "poverty of misery and utter neediness," as Johannes Metz points out.[1] This is the way Jesus lived while on earth, and this is what he teaches us to learn from him as recorded in the gospels (Mt 11:29).

Jesus teaches his disciples through Paul: "Abraham believed and hoped, even when there was no reason for hoping, and so became 'the father of many nations' " (Rm 4:18). We are to respond to the great dignity to which we are called by hoping that what is impossible to us is possible to God. We disciples are taught by Jesus to hope in God's power when all seems impossible according to our strength. We are to give everything to God in each moment and thus experience the paradox of true living: "Whoever tries to gain his own life will lose it, but whoever loses his life for my sake will gain it" (Mt 10:39).

2. Mark 10:35-45

In this text the disciples James and John, the sons of Zebedee, request out of prideful ambition to be granted the highest places of honor, "to sit, one at your right hand and one at your left, in your glory" (Mk 10:36). In Matthew 20:26-28 we find that it is the mother of James and John that requests this honor of Jesus. The ten disciples became very indignant toward the sons of Zebedee, no doubt because they also wanted to have places of honor in the coming of the kingdom, which they saw as one of temporal glory and power. Thus, Jesus teaches them and us modern disciples about true discipleship:

> You know that those who are supposed to rule over the Gentiles lord it over them, and their great men exercise authority over them. But it shall not be so among you; but whoever would be great among you must be your servant, and whoever would be first among you must be slave of all. For the Son of man also came not to be served but to serve, and to give his life as a ransom for many. (Mk 10:42-45)

Jesus is teaching us also that those who have authority within the loving community of the Church must not use it with personal ambition, but rather in the performance of their leadership by *diakonia* or humble service to the other members of the Body. He calls our attention to himself, who served by being a "ransom" for us to take away our sins.

Jesus insists that not only servants but also leaders should be "slaves" of all, even while they exercise their God-given authority. They need to exercise this authority without any self-pride or self-interest, but rather in loving dedication. They need to help each member of the Body to attain his or her potential to also become a humble servant.

3. Luke 9:16; Matthew 18:3

In these two texts we find Christ enunciate to his disciples the basic principle as to what truly constitutes greatness in the kingdom of God. Both Luke and Matthew present the disciples as approaching Jesus after they have been discussing who was the greatest among the twelve of them. Jesus places a child at his side and answered them:

> Whoever receives this child in my name receives me, and whoever receives me receives him who sent me; for he who is least among you all is the one who is great. (Lk 9:48; Mt 18:2-4)

Here Jesus teaches that in heaven as on earth the sign of greatness is the mindset of being humble before God and neighbor, as all members of the Body of Christ lovingly seek to serve others with *agapic* love. Thus Jesus teaches that those possess true greatness who have a childlike sense of littleness, and therefore show that they belong to the free children of God.

4. Matthew 23:11

Here Matthew repeats what he had written in 18:1-4 about who is the greatest among the disciples. But in this text Jesus is teaching his disciples to avoid the hypocrisy of the Pharisees and the scribes. To do this they must become servants.

> He who is greatest among you shall be your servant; whoever exalts himself will be humbled, and whoever humbles himself will be exalted. (Mt 23:11-12)

5. John 13:4-17

Here is John's summary of Jesus' teaching as to who is the greatest in God's kingdom. In a parabolic gesture, Jesus washes the feet of his disciples as though he were a mere servant, he who is the Master. He then teaches them:

> You call me Teacher and Lord, and it is right that you do so, because that is what I am. I, your Lord and Teacher, have just washed your feet. You, then, should wash one another's feet. I have set an example for you. I am telling you the truth: no slave is greater than his master, and no messenger is greater than the one who sent him. Now that you know this truth, how happy you will be if you put it into practice. (Jn 13:13-17)

God's kenotic love

Jesus points out that his washing of the disciples' feet shows his superiority over them as their Master and Teacher; it is his supreme freedom which prompts him to perform the humblest task of a slave, so that his disciples and those who will follow them will "know" how great his love is for them. Peter does not understand the meaning of Jesus' actions, but Jesus explains: "What I intend to do you do not understand right now, but you will understand by and by" (Jn 13:7). Peter and other Christians would understand only through the outpouring of the Holy Spirit after Jesus' death and resurrection.

That understanding embraces two truths absolutely essential to living the true Christian life. The first is that Jesus shows that he in human form images the triune God from all eternity in choosing a life of loving service on behalf of others. God's love for us is a *kenotic* or self-emptying love. This love Jesus images by his total availability, by his mutuality in sharing himself as our equal, and by his complete gift of himself out of love for us unto death.

What is God like? He is like Jesus, who is the "image of the unseen God" (Col 1:15). How does God love us? He loves us in the way Jesus images that perfect love for us. In the Last Supper Jesus opens his loving heart to his disciples. It is a humble heart that wishes to serve as a slave. Jesus bends down and washes the feet of Peter and John, Judas and the other disciples. The heart of God never bent lower to touch his children than in that gesture of humble service. The primary meaning of this gesture, beyond the example Jesus gives for his disciples' imitation, is that he is the image of God's divine power placed at the service of us human beings. "My Father goes on working, and so do I!" (Jn 5:17).

In Paul's hymn in Philippians 2:6-10, Jesus, one with God, did not deem this an honor to hold on to but "emptied himself." Jesus did not give up his divinity in becoming human, but, more positively, he became a most perfect expression of it. He reveals that at the heart of all reality is the triune community of loving persons, who live for each other. It is an *I* and a *Thee* in a *We* community, constituted by the bonding, hidden love of the Spirit. It is based on *ek-stasis*, the ecstasy of standing beyond or outside of oneself, in order to move toward others in self-giving. It means to be "othered into new levels of personhood" by living for the other. It is emptying love which brings true fulfillment, as the gift of oneself comes back to birth the giver into true *I-ness* through the gift of the beloved.

Servants to others

Jesus chose the symbol of washing his disciples' feet with water to indicate a complete, comprehensive cleansing of all our worldly values, so as to live as he lived (cf. 1 Jn 1:7).

The proof that we are disciples of Christ and truly "saved," must lie in our readiness to give away our beautifully transformed selves in humble, loving service to others. We live this in utter *availability, mutuality,* and *self-gift,* just as Jesus became the servant of us all, especially in shedding his blood. Jesus experienced the complete outpouring love of the Father through his Spirit. He chose a human style of life that best reflected his return of love, or better, the transformation he experienced in becoming the beautiful, beloved Son through his Father's love.

So as we experience the infinite, emptying, serving love of the indwelling Trinity for us, we too should live for others in self-sacrificing service. Following Jesus means to be washed thoroughly of all our desires for power and domination to live as he lived: as a humble, suffering servant.

6. Luke 18:9-14

Jesus gives this teaching as a parable that he tells at the banquet table of the Pharisee. It is directed at those "who trusted in themselves that they were righteous and despised others" (Lk 18:9).

> Two men went up into the temple to pray, one a Pharisee and the other a tax collector. The Pharisee stood and prayed thus with himself, "God, I thank thee that I am not like other men, extortioners, unjust, adulterers, or even like this tax collector. I fast twice a week, I give tithes of all that I get." But the tax collector, standing far off, would not even lift up his eyes to heaven, but beat his breast, saying, "God, be merciful to me a sinner!" I tell you, this man went down to his house justified rather than the other, for everyone who exalts himself will be humbled, but he who humbles himself will be exalted. (Lk 18:9-14)

Jesus contrasts the inner dispositions of the Pharisee and the publican. Publicans were despised "sinners," tax collectors for the Romans, and hated for cheating their own Jewish people of their money. The Pharisee was full of pride and self-conceit. He observed externally the laws of fasting, tithing and saying prayers. But he placed his claim to righteousness not to a humble, contrite conversion within his heart, but to the works he did. In a word, he considered himself a holy person because of the external works that others saw him do. But he had little true love for God or neighbor, as he considered himself superior to others whom he branded as sinners, especially the publican in the back of the synagogue.

The publican sinner, aware of his sinful state, prays humbly with his eyes cast down before the majesty of God, as he strikes his breast and begs God's mercy on account of his sins. Jesus says that the sinner was justified, but that the Pharisee was not. The reason Jesus gives repeats his continued teaching, as we have already seen: "Everyone who exalts himself will be humbled, but he who humbles himself will be exalted" (Lk 18:14).

Summary

In the gospels' presentation of his teaching on humility, we see Jesus living a style of life which he wants all those to live who follow him. If we are humble, we will not exalt ourselves through distorted pride, but we will recognize the privilege to serve others in order to grow more in the likeness of Jesus, our Master.

It is to experience the paradox that Jesus repeats in all four gospels: the necessity to lose our life, our present motivation so often distorted by false pride, in order to find our true life in God's divine love. He assures us that if we become poor, humble servants toward others, we lose what is false and unreal in our lives and become exalted by God and full of imperishable riches. We serve God and each other, and this sets us free from all selfish pride, helping us to enjoy even now the true freedom of the Holy Spirit (2 Co 3:18).

We need to embrace Jesus' teaching on the necessity to acquire humility and to study his example. He was obedient unto his death on the cross. We will take serious his teaching by living it, for he is our way, truth and life (Jn 14:6).

The above texts do not exhaust Jesus' teaching on humility. But they present this ever-recurring virtue and our need to cultivate it. If you and I, like his first disciples, desire to enter into God's kingdom and enjoy a high and intense union with God-Trinity, we must not seek to be exalted but to be little as children. We must be humble as servants, humble as Jesus was and still wishes to be in and through you and me and all of his disciples living on this earth.

That must be our constant prayer, as we joyfully strive in every moment to be like Mary, the Mother of Jesus:

> He has remembered me, his lowly servant. . . . He has stretched out his mighty arm and scattered the proud with all their plans. He has brought down mighty kings from their thrones, and lifted up the lowly. He has filled the hungry with good things, and sent the rich away with empty hands. (Lk 1:48, 51-53)

In the kingdom of God true greatness is true humility. This may seem like abasement and degradation to the world, but to God it is to be God-like. In fact, God in Jesus Christ lived as a servant for all of his created beings, teaching us to be humble servants of each other. Truly, God's power is not of this world; that would be no real power at all. Jesus humbled himself, and the Father exalted him. He lost his life, only to find it in and through his death and resurrection. He became a humble servant who died so that we might be exalted in our lowly service of love toward others and even now share in his glory.

Like attracts like. Jesus lived humbly and served us. He taught us over and over the necessity of learning from him how to become gentle and humble of heart (Mt 11:9). What

Jesus is he wishes to give us, as he draws us into greater oneness with him and the Father through the Spirit's gift of humility.

A Humble Life Hidden in Christ Jesus

An important reality to understand for us Christians is that in his earthly life Jesus was totally like us. He was the pre-existent Word of God that became flesh. Yet, he lived most of his earthly life in obscurity in the small, insignificant town of Nazareth as the son of a humble carpenter, Joseph.

He was as human as you and I are and, therefore, he was subject to the same human laws of growth. "And Jesus increased in wisdom, in stature, and in favor with God and men" (Lk 2:52). He had a human body, as you have, with its physical and psychic parts. He hungered and thirsted, required sleep, had sexual powers which he needed to discipline, along with intellectual, emotional and volitional endowments: "We have one who has been tempted in every way that we are, though he is without sin" (Heb 4:15).

We can learn much about our developing genuine humility by contemplating Jesus in his thirty years of hidden life at Nazareth. If we do so frequently, we can learn God's values over the values of the world: "Now the life you have is hidden with Christ in God" (Col 3:3). Jesus teaches us in what human greatness consists through his humble birth in a cave at Bethlehem, his simple life at Nazareth, and his public life as narrated in the gospels, leading to his hour of death on the cross.

Learning humility through integration

If we judge by the worldly standards of both the society of Jesus' times as well as our own, Jesus was "getting nowhere fast." Buried away in an insignificant corner of Galilee, Jesus

57

lived a life of complete surrender in love to his heavenly Father. He had to learn to live humanly with his own divinity, he who was "one with God from all eternity" (Ph 2:6). He had to discover the presence of God in every facet of his humanity, and to yield that part of his being in loving obedience to his Father.

He had to learn to let God be the source of his being, as he tempered his human will to the divine power that was at his command. His human hands would touch a leper and heal him, and that experience of using his hands in loving touch was an experience he had to acquire. His human voice would cry out in love, and Lazarus would come forth from the tomb.

His human intelligence pondering over the scriptures of his ancestors in his village synagogue would be the instrument for communicating God's divine message to human beings. He had to study that message and experience it in the depths of his entire human being.

His task at Nazareth

This is the task which unfolded during Jesus' hidden years at Nazareth. He had to grow into a personality that would be fully realized and human. Yet he had to grow totally submissive to the divine Father, whom he progressively experienced in his humanity as dwelling intimately within him, making him and the Father one in diversity (Jn 17:21). Tradition tells us that Jesus left Nazareth about his thirtieth year of life. We are amazed that he had so quickly accomplished his task of integrating divinity and humanity.

Jesus was not wasting his time or merely going through the stages of becoming a mature human being. He was preparing every day for the redemption of the world! He was learning how to be totally human before God. Within the Trinity, God cannot be "humble of heart." Only we human beings acquire an understanding of humility by experiencing our finiteness and existential limitations. We are not God but a created being that receives existence and all power from him.

But through the unbelievable "good news" of the mystery of the incarnation, the Word has become flesh and now can mirror for us human beings perfect humility of God. This is what Jesus must have meant when he invited all human beings to come and learn of him, because he is meek and humble of heart (Mt 11:29).

Learn of me

What happened at Nazareth is a pattern of what must happen in us. We have God-Trinity dwelling within us. God, the Father, Son and Holy Spirit, have united themselves to our humanity. While on this earth, our principal task is to progressively learn how to discover within us and outside of us this indwelling Trinity, who works dynamically for us with their uncreated energies of love.

We are to see God shining transparently from within the depths of our being. "Didn't you realize that you were God's temple and that the Spirit of God was living among you? If anybody should destroy the temple of God, God will destroy him, because the temple of God is sacred, and you are that temple" (1 Co 3:16-17).

We are called to a lifelong Nazareth experience, where we explore or at least seek to explore the deepest parts of ourselves in which God-Trinity dwells. Since there is no limit to this union, we will never reach a fullness of intimacy or self-surrender to the Trinity. We have to learn how to use our imagination, intellect, emotions, will, sexuality—our entire body-soul-spirit being—as a humble, loving gift to God, who is intimately present and gives himself to us as Father, Son and Spirit.

If God is present within us, he is there as activated energies of love. He moves within us with his personal love relationships as Father, Son and Holy Spirit. If we believe this, we can experience a divine movement within our lives through our continued, humble response. This response is in some limited way comparable to the one Jesus gave to his heavenly Father, in and through the Holy Spirit, throughout his entire earthly life: "Not my will, but yours be done."

The goal of our lives

Jesus teaches us through his humanity that the goal of our lives is to move freely according to the inspirations of the Holy Spirit, who dwells within us and brings us into complete and humble obedience to Jesus Christ and his heavenly Father. It is to structure and discipline our body, soul and spirit relationships, so that we move in the power of the Spirit through the Son directly to the Father. This can be expressed briefly as humble familiarity with God.

The humanity of Jesus acquired this familiarity at Nazareth. Jesus moved his human consciousness and all his human powers directly through the indwelling Spirit to total oneness with the Father, by humbly surrendering to live only to glorify the Father. In his humanity Jesus became one with his divinity, which brought him into oneness with the Father through the same Holy Spirit.

You and I are not divine by nature; but by God's permeating, uncreated energies of love, which we can call "primal grace," we are called to be "participators of God's own nature" (2 P 1:4). Our aim in life is to join our humanity into oneness with the permeating, divine, triune Persons who dwell within us. This means having the ability to easily find God in all things. It means sensitivity to his presence, contentedness in abiding in God, humble docility to all the movements of his Spirit.

It also means a straight and truthful movement of our intentions toward pleasing God with every thought, word and deed. It means that we allow ourselves to be caught up in the current of God's powerful love, which flows strongly and gently through our lives. It means that we have "interior eyes" to see how all events, even those that the world may label insignificant or unpleasant, can be exciting moments, which unveil the loving presence of God and allow us to become always more participators in God's own divine nature.

This is the goal of our lives. The growth is slow and sometimes painful. But if we realize that in growing toward this goal we are imitating in a very profound way our Lord, then we will joyously and generously try to do so.

A poor and simple life

Jesus shows us how he learned to become humble of heart through the style of life he led in those obscure years of his earthly life at Nazareth. He lived a poor and simple life. In a town like Nazareth during the time of Jesus, the villagers lived with only the mere necessities. But Jesus' poverty was more than physical. He entered into a psychic and spiritual poverty in his humanity, which reflected his basic, divine attitude toward his heavenly Father within the Trinity.

As the eternal Son of God, he realized that everything he possessed was sheer gift from the love of the Father. In his humanity, Jesus continually reflected this relationship. And according to his likeness all of us have been created. Throughout his earthly life Jesus experienced daily that he was most radically and ontologically non-being, except for the love which God poured out in his unselfish creation.

Jesus lived poverty as he experienced, through the Father's Spirit, the riches which God first poured out into his humanity. This poverty became for him a humble recognition of

God's sovereignty and free gift of love. This permanent attitude of mind Jesus assumed toward himself, his Father, and each person he met. It is a poverty that can truly be called humility. In his human creation Jesus is nothing but "an empty receptacle to be filled with God's goodness," as Irenaeus of the second century says.

His Father is all to him. The Son grows in the human experience of every moment to become "meek and humble of heart" (Mt 11:29). Jesus surrenders himself to do whatever the Father wishes him to do, both at Nazareth and finally on the cross.

Jesus was poor. He lived as a carpenter in a small village. For his food and shelter he was dependent on the offering of others for services rendered. He was not destitute or heroic in his poverty. But he was absolutely poor, because no *thing* possessed him. He was possessed exclusively by his Father, and so he used things only as an external expression of that inner emptiness before the allness of his Father.

A life of hard work

There are few of us who escape from having to earn a living by our work. Before the first man had fallen through disobedience, God had already given to him the command to take this created world and fashion it into a song of praise to its Creator: "Be fruitful, multiply, fill the earth and conquer. Be masters of the fish of the sea, the birds of heaven and all living animals on the earth" (Gn 1:28). Yet, we often find our work not very creative. We do not always seem to develop ourselves or the universe into something noble and creative. All too often our work becomes banal, monotonous and boring.

The life of Jesus hidden away in a carpenter shop at Nazareth could hardly be called creative and exciting in the sense of modern psychology. Jesus had to labor diligently for the simple things that he and his family needed to sustain them-selves in life. The power that he had at hand was his own brawn and muscle. He had to sweat much in the Galilean heat.

And what was his recreation after a full day's work? He did not have any of the modern devices that amuse and recreate us. His life was one continuous round of monotonous duties. At night there was the glow of a candle or small oil lamp for a few hours more, until he fell into sleep only to return to the same work the next day.

One with our twentieth-century mentality might ask: "Where was he going with his life? One day yielded to the next; one year to the other. The same neighbors, the same work, the same food. Stagnation had surely set in!" Yet, it was the interior spirit of Jesus that transformed what appeared to be a life of no great creativity into a life of infinite beauty and value before his heavenly Father: "He who sent me is with me and has not left me to myself, for I always do what pleases him" (Jn 8:29).

The Spirit in Jesus allowed him to grow in each activity and event "in wisdom, in stature, and in favor with God and men" (Lk 2:52). All anxiety and boredom were removed by his openness to meet his loving Father in each fresh moment. The situation was not objectified as either holy or profane, pleasant or unpleasant, worthwhile or worthless. But from the inner presence of the Spirit of love, he moved freely through life's events and circumstances to respond fully according to the Father's mind. His life, made up of his free choice within each moment, brought him into a growing experience that in all things he was the Word, one with the mind of the Father.

Free from sin and self-seeking, Jesus was also free to be loved infinitely by his Father, and to strive through his daily work to joyfully return that love.

Work was a humble way of acting out his devotion to the Father; each action was important, as he labored in all things to please him. Every moment was a labor of love, a song of self-surrender.

Jesus was obedient

One of the chief characteristics of authentic humility is obedience. We read in Luke's gospel: "Jesus then went down with them and came to Nazareth and lived under their authority" (2:51). Like any other Jewish child of that time, Jesus lived day by day acting upon the slightest wish or command of Joseph and Mary. And in that obedience he discovered the wish of his heavenly Father. Not that the Father was leading him exactly as those in authority around him commanded him. Yet, he knew that he would discover the Father in those social relationships, as he accepted his place in the society of his family and their town.

God loved his material world and sent his only begotten Son to become forever a part of it through the incarnation. Thus Jesus knew that the material world, especially the interaction of human beings, would be the "place" where his heavenly Father would speak to him of his eternal love, and allow Jesus to freely make his return of love to the Father. Jesus was obedient to others in legitimate authority, because in his gentle spirit he was always present to the Father who spoke to him through others. The Father was greater than he, and without the Father the Son could do nothing (Jn 5:30; 14:28).

Yet, Jesus was no automaton. He had to search to discover what would be most pleasing to the Father. This brought him into an obedience to the Father by obeying others. In the depths of his heart, of his innermost consciousness, Jesus touched the *Holy*. He breathed, smiled, laughed and cried in the holy presence of his infinitely loving Father. All created beings, touching Jesus in new, surprising experiences, were received as gifts by that delicate, sensitive gentleness in him. When Jesus gave himself up to obey others, it was a joyful act of freedom to take his life in hand and return it totally and freely to his Father. Seeking only his Father's will, Jesus was able to obey others, because he sought only to obey his Father.

The prayer of Jesus

Jesus' life on this earth teaches us that his humility grew mostly as he daily experienced in prayer the gift of the Father in his Spirit of love. Jesus lived what he taught his disciples: "But when you pray, go to your private room and, when you have shut your door, pray to your Father who is in that secret place, and your Father who sees all that is done in secret will reward you" (Mt 6:6).

At Nazareth Jesus learned to pray in the sense of always walking in the communicating presence of his Father. He sought to bring his consciousness in loving surrender to the consciousness of the Father, who was always present, seeking communion with his Son through his Spirit of love.

Jesus teaches us, therefore, that prayer is fundamentally a listening to God, as he continually communicates his love to us at each moment. We pray when we are "attentive" to the presence of God, when we lift up our heart and mind to God's communicating presence. God does not begin and then cease to enter into this self-giving. At Nazareth Jesus realized that the Father surrounded him at every moment of his earthly existence with his Spirit.

He opened himself humbly to receive that "invasion" of his Father by yielding actively to whatever the Father was asking of him at each moment. Thus Jesus prayed always in whatever he was doing. He had to discover each day that his very activities were to be that "secret place" where he was to tune in to the Father's loving presence. Unlike us, who so often find our work a distraction that takes us away from being attentive to the presence of God, Jesus always received the loving penetration of his Father.

In such a state of inner attentiveness to the Father's loving energies, Jesus learned that true prayer is ultimately union of his will with that of the Father. At Nazareth he learned in his humanity that the quality of his prayer was not measured by how great he felt in prayer, but rather how surrendered in humility he was in his will-determination to be total gift back to the Father.

Prayer became not an activity that Jesus engaged in before he did something else, but it was a state of being, turned inwardly toward the Father at every moment in loving adoration and self-surrender. Prayer became synonymous with humble love. "My son, give me your heart" (Pr 23:26).

A trinitarian community

Jesus preached that eternal life was in knowing the indwelling community of Father and Son in the Spirit of love: "And eternal life is this: to know you, the only true God, and Jesus Christ whom you have sent" (Jn 17:3). Therefore, through God's Word incarnate, the one "nearest the heart of the Father" (Jn 1:18), God reveals to us his inner life. By his death and resurrection, this revealing Word, Jesus Christ, is now a *living* Word, dwelling within us along with his Holy Spirit.

Jesus not only *gives* us the elements that constitute God's inner life as he experienced them in his prayer at Nazareth and throughout his entire life, but he makes it possible through his Spirit for us to *experience* those elements.

This trinitarian community of Father, Son and Holy Spirit, constantly communicating itself to us at all times, is at the heart of all reality. You are a gift of that love. Your life is to more and more share with Jesus at Nazareth that mystery of love, that you may humbly share the secret of God's very own intimate life. Jesus shows you this reality as the spirit of Nazareth. Your life is to be one with that of Jesus of Nazareth, hidden in the tremendous reality of God's triune, personalized love for you at each moment. Paul beautifully summarizes the goal of our humility, especially seen in our intimate prayer life before the indwelling Trinity:

Let your thoughts be on heavenly things, not on the things of the earth, because you have died and now the life you have is hidden with Christ in God. But when Christ is revealed and he is your life, you too will be revealed in all your glory with him. (Col 3:3)

Jesus, Humble Servant

Feodor Dostoyevsky wrote a classical novel, called *The Idiot*. His biographers tell us that he rewrote the ending ten times, for he tried to portray the most Christ-like human being he could imagine. Prince Myshkin in the novel was considered by many to have been insane, but the children, who loved him, never thought he was anyone but a beautiful, gentle, humble, loving man. After he is declared "sane" and returns from Switzerland to his native country of Russia, he continues his Christ-like, gentle ways in a society of so-called "normal" people. In the end the author has his hero return to his form of "insanity."

A mad generosity

Jesus came among human beings and showed himself to be gentle and kind. He told his followers, against the decadent religious leaders of his time, that they were to give away their lives for love of one another. He was the "friend of sinners" and went about doing good to all, even to those who hated him and plotted his death. To any sick or disturbed person he brought comfort and healing. He was meek and humble and wanted no part of Caesar's power. The only power he possessed was the humility to love each person who came into his life. He touched the crowds, listened to their anxieties, forgave their sins. He lived only to bring life, and that more abundantly, to all who wanted it. He was total availability to all who needed him.

He had few disciples, because many who heard him preach

Thank you for choosing this book.
If you would like to receive regular information
about New City Press titles, please fill in this card.

Title purchased: _____

_____

Please check the subjects
that are of particular interest to you:

☐ **FATHERS OF THE CHURCH**

☐ **CLASSICS IN SPIRITUALITY**

☐ **CONTEMPORARY SPIRITUALITY**

☐ **THEOLOGY**

☐ **SCRIPTURE AND COMMENTARIES**

☐ **FAMILY LIFE**

☐ **BIOGRAPHY / HISTORY**

Other subjects of interest: _____

_____

Name:_____

Address: _____

_____

thought he was mad. Many, like the rich young man (Mk 10:17-22), walked away when he suggested the crazy idea that those who were wealthy should go and sell everything they had, give the money to the poor and follow him. He was the most "impractical" person. People were not to worry about what they would eat or put on, but they were to seek the kingdom of heaven. But then he did not even have a pillow upon which to put his head at night. His disciples were to love everyone, even those who hated them. But really! And then he insisted:

> Bless those who curse you, pray for those who treat you badly. To the man who slaps you on one cheek, present the other cheek too; to the man who takes your cloak from you, do not refuse your tunic. Give to everyone who asks you, and do not ask for your property back from the man who robs you. Treat others as you would like them to treat you. If you love those who love you, what thanks can you expect? For even sinners do that much. And if you lend to those from whom you hope to receive, what thanks can you expect? Even sinners lend to sinners to get back the same amount. Instead love your enemies and do good, and lend without any hope of return. . . . Give and there will be gifts for you; a full measure, pressed down, shaken together, and running over, will be poured into your lap; because the amount you measure out is the amount you will be given back. (Lk 6:28-38)

Learn of me, for I am humble of heart

The disciples were to learn from Jesus who was meek and humble of heart (Mt 11:29). This would require a continued conversion of heart and the power of God's grace to put on his mind (Eph 4:17). We were to visit the sick, the lonely, those

deadly murderers in prison and tell them that we loved them.
We were to give and give, even losing our lives for others. We
were to hate, even our parents, brothers and sisters, if they
were an obstacle to following him. We were to be humble
servants to everyone we meet, washing their feet, binding up
their wounds, meeting all their needs.

And all that he asked of his disciples, he did himself. When
he washed the feet of his disciples, he summarized who he
was. He was the "image of God": "Who sees me, sees the
Father" (Jn 14:9). He was *Ebed Yahweh*, God's servant, suffering
for his people. He was conscious that everything he did came
from his Father. He lived only to please him and bring him
glory. Over and over he confessed that he was nothing, while
his Father was all. He served the Father, taking nothing unto
himself.

In a series of "not I," Jesus asserts his humble role as servant
before his Father:

> The Son can do nothing by himself; he can do only what
> he sees the Father doing; and whatever the Father does,
> the Son does too. (Jn 5:19)

> I can do nothing by myself; I can only judge as I am told
> to judge. . . . As for human approval, this means nothing
> to me. (Jn 5:30, 41)

> . . . because I have come from heaven, not to do my own
> will, but to do the will of the one who sent me. (Jn 7:16)
> Yet I have not come of myself, no, there is one who sent
> me and I really come from him. (Jn 7:28)

> Not that I care for my own glory, there is someone who
> takes care of that and is the judge of it. (Jn 8:50)

> And my word is not my own: it is the word of the one
> who sent me. (Jn 14:24)

Totally dependent upon the Father

In these statements, Jesus reveals an inner consciousness of his ultimate worth and meaning as a human being that derives from his complete dependence on the Father. There is no vanity or self-seeking in his words or actions. His primal motivation is to serve the wishes of his heavenly Father. He lives in the presence of his Father. But that Father is constantly working, out of love for him and the whole universe.

"My Father goes on working, and so do I" (Jn 5:17). As the Father loves him (Jn 15:9) and serves him in all things, so Jesus loves and serves us.

The suffering servant

Jesus and his early disciples were aware that his whole mission in life was to serve the Father's will. But as the Father's will unfolded, Christ became ever more conscious that his was a service on behalf of God's people. In God's eternal plan, this service would bring Jesus to make a free gift of himself on behalf of the human race. Jesus knew that eventually the Good Shepherd would lay down his life for all human beings.

The *kerygma* or preaching of the early Church, as found in the gospels and Pauline writings, clearly attests to the necessity of Jesus to serve unto humiliating death so that he might enter into glory. On Pentecost, Peter preached: "For this reason the whole house of Israel can be certain that God has made this Jesus whom you crucified both Lord and Christ" (Ac 2:36).

Jesus explained patiently to the two disciples on the road to Emmaus:

> You foolish men! So slow to believe the full message of the prophets! Was it not ordained that the Christ should suffer and so enter into his glory? (Lk 24:36)

When Jesus was baptized by John in the Jordan, he humbled himself to be reckoned among sinners. He heard his Father's voice from heaven: "This is my Son, the Beloved; my favor rests on him" (Mt 3:17). This is the introduction to the first song of the servant of Yahweh: "Here is my servant whom I uphold, my chosen one in whom my soul delights" (Is 42:1).

We learn why Jesus gives pleasure to the Father: He has come to serve, not to be served. And his ultimate service will be to surrender his life for all of us to ransom us back from the kingdom of sin and death (Mt 20:29; Mk 10:45). John the Baptist gives this early Christian teaching when he declares, "Look, there is the lamb of God that takes away the sin of the world" (Jn 1:29). John the Evangelist, who makes much of the parallelism between Jesus and the Passover Lamb, surely must have had in mind the lamb-like characteristics that Deutero-Isaiah attributed to Yahweh's servant:

> Harshly dealt with, he bore it humbly, he never opened his mouth, like a lamb that is led to the slaughter-house, like a sheep that is dumb before its shearers, never opening its mouth. (Is 53:7)

He takes upon himself our suffering

Jesus, the suffering servant, would fulfill the prophecy of Deutero-Isaiah in being a victim on our behalf. He is not a victim of circumstances, turned over to the wiles of those who persecuted him. There is a plan of propitiation for the sins of the human race. He would somehow bear the sins of the world and take them away, as John the Evangelist notes. Isaiah depicted the suffering servant of Yahweh in similar terms.

> And yet ours were the sufferings he bore,
> ours the sorrows he carried.

But we, we thought of him as someone punished,
struck by God, and brought low.
Yet he was pierced through for our faults,
Crushed for our sins,
On him lies a punishment that brings us peace,
And through his wounds we are healed.

(Isaiah 53:4-5)

The kenosis of Jesus

The outstanding scriptural text that links Jesus' death on the
cross with a humble obedience to the Father is the famous
early Christian hymn that Paul presents in Philippians 2:6-11.
Paul implies Jesus' free choice, not only to be the servant, but
to go all the way, obedient to the Father's decree to give
himself over to death. From such an emptying (in Greek,
kenosis) he would be exalted in glory by the Father.

His state was divine,
yet he did not cling
to his equality with God
but emptied himself
to assume the condition of a slave,
and to become as men are;
and being as all men are,
he was humbler yet,
even to accepting death,
death on a cross.
But God raised him high
and gave him the name
which is above all other names
so that all beings in the heavens,
on earth and in the underworld,

should bend the knee at the name of Jesus
and that every tongue should acclaim
Jesus Christ as Lord,
to the glory of God the Father.

(Philippians 2:6-11)

In this passage we note the Christian community's profession of faith in Jesus' divinity. He was equal with God, but he surrendered the glory, the *shekinah,* of God's powerful presence in him. He did this so that he could in all things be like us. "God dealt with sin by sending his own Son in a body as physical as any sinful body, and in that body God condemned sin" (Rm 8:3). He was tempted as we are (Heb 4:15). His love for us was so great that there was nothing to distinguish him from ordinary people. He was a carpenter. He knew hunger, thirst and fatigue. He grew in human knowledge. He learned how to make things and how to cope with life's problems. Above all, he learned how to experience his Father's love in the love he received and gave to the women and men who came into his life as his friends.

And yet, as he grew in consciousness of who he was and what the Father was asking of him, he continually rejected his own will in complete submission and obedience to his Father's will. He disregarded the shamefulness of the cross, enduring it for love of us (Heb 12:2). For this reason the Father exalted him, giving him the name of Lord of the universe, allowing him to be called by the name no man could utter—*vere Deus,* truly God, Yahweh.

The logic of humble love

I often ask myself: But why the cross? Could God not have been pleased with Jesus merely *living* in that lowly state as man and servant? Even if a blood offering were humanly the most basic symbol of total giving, could not the human race have been redeemed by one drop from the Lamb of God? Why such a prodigality of self-emptying, to the point of complete dehumanization? Jesus empties himself not only of his divine glory, but he goes further still by emptying himself of all control over his human existence.

This utter emptying on the cross was foreseen by the prophet Isaiah in describing the peak of humble service on the part of Yahweh's suffering servant:

> Like a sapling he grew up in front of us,
> like a root in arid ground.
> Without beauty, without majesty (we saw him),
> no looks to attract our eyes;
> a thing despised and rejected by men,
> a man of sorrows and familiar with suffering,
> a man to make people screen their faces;
> he was despised and we took no account of him,
> and yet ours were the sufferings he bore,
> ours the sorrows he carried.
> But we, we thought of him as someone punished,
> struck by God, and brought low.

(Isaiah 53:2-4)

But the terrifying suffering he underwent for us in Gethsemane and on Calvary cannot be understood only theologically and explained by a legalistic atonement theory. According to such thinking, God's justice demanded repayment by the suffering God-man to atone for our human sinfulness. There must be more that the word of God reveals to us, as we comtemplate Christ's humble suffering. Something that only his Holy Spirit can reveal to us, far beyond the reach of our intellects.

Three degrees of humility

Just as we know various degrees of acting out the love we have for another, so Jesus grew in his humility and freedom to surrender himself more and more completely to the Father. We return love to the degree that we have experienced being loved. In his long hours of solitary communion with the Father, Jesus must have progressively experienced ever deeper assurances of the Father's infinite love for him. If mystics could lose consciousness under the rapture of God's flaming love for them, how must Jesus have experienced the Father's fiery love for him, poured over him, filling him with light, "Light from Light"?

Jesus experienced in prayerful communion his heavenly Father's immense love for him—especially at his baptism, during the forty days alone in the desert and his all-night vigils on mountain tops, during his public ministry, agonizing in the Garden of Gethsemane, and in the dying moments on the cross. Through these experiences he grew more sensitive to what love was asking by way of a returned self-oblation.

Much has been written about the psychological development of Jesus' human consciousness.[1] But the gospels are an interpretation of the early Christian community's faith experience concerning the person of Jesus Christ. And therefore we are always left uncertain as to which words attributed to Jesus were really spoken by him and what was his psychological state of consciousness at any stage of his human development. I believe that the following theological approach can gain for us nuanced insights into Jesus' redemptive service on our behalf.

Love is humble self-sacrifice

It is clear from our experience of human love that the basic level of love and self-sacrifice is wanting to do whatever the one we love wishes or commands. Throughout his human existence, Jesus must have been at one with all the pious Jews of his day, who strove diligently to return God's love by remembering his commandments and observing them with perfect care. He surely realized during his public life that it would be necessary for him to suffer and die. He knew clearly, therefore, that the Father was calling him to give up his life freely for our sakes. And yet, obeying his Father's commands was no little sacrifice, as his agony in the garden proves:

> "Father," he said, "if you are willing, take this cup away from me. Nevertheless, let your will be done, not mine. . . ." In his anguish he prayed even more earnestly and his sweat fell to the ground like great drops of blood. (Lk 22:42-44)

Humility seeks to give more

Still, his love prompted him to want to give more. Jesus was sensitive to his Father's loving presence, and he desired to be a loving presence to his Father.

Just as we do in our lives, Jesus made free choices in response to the presence of his Father. These choices were made sometimes very spontaneously, other times with reflection, still other times in deep, silent prayer. Here we see a more delicate discernment of the will of his Father. Not only does Jesus seek to do whatever his Father would command him to do, but he seeks to act out his return of love by being sensitive to the slightest wish the Father expresses in any given situation. It requires greater love and humility, delicacy and discernment to ask what the wish of the Father might be in one or another circumstance, rather than merely seeking to fulfill his great commands. Jesus moved under the power of the Spirit in greater submission and surrender.

Yet, Jesus grew also in going beyond the wishes of the Father, seeking in all things to please him. Even in human love we can from time to time forget ourselves and, in a burst of self-sacrifice for the one we love, "improvise" some immense gift of love. Love is there, within our hearts. We make a freely chosen sacrifice, under no obligation through an expressed command or even a wish on the part of the one we love. Jesus Christ, who had experienced in his humanity the love of the Father as no other person on earth had, sought to please his Father. He wanted to please him who gave all things to him, to make him happy. And so Jesus could say these words and, more importantly, live according to them:

> He who sent me is with me,
> and has not left me to myself,
> for I always do what pleases him.

> (John 8:29)

Creative love

Much in the life of Christ, especially the terrifying suffering in his passion and death, can be explained in his free choice to imitate the outpouring love of total self-giving of the Father to his Son. I like to call it "creative suffering" or "creative humility." It is what keeps love alive. It is fire touching dry wood and making it turn into fire also. Loved infinitely by the Father, Jesus was being driven in his human consciousness, not by any obligation but by a consuming desire, to take his life into his hands and give it back to his beloved Father.

Given that he was the Word of the Father made flesh, we could say that Jesus *had* to pour himself out, or he would have done psychic and spiritual harm to his nature. In emptying himself by a free choice to suffer more and more, Jesus was becoming the image of his heavenly Father. Going all the way, even unto death, he was becoming the Word, God's infinite, loving presence, telling us that God the Father loves us perfectly and completely in the perfect image of his love: the humble, suffering and dying Jesus.

Perhaps now the suffering servant becomes better understood. There is light in the darkness of Jesus' *kenosis*. It is not merely that he *had* to die in order to save us from eternal death. Throughout his whole life Jesus freely chooses to descend into the heart of each of us human beings. He chooses to descend into the suffering, dying heart of humanity. He freely wishes to become the poorest of the poor, the loneliest of all lonely human beings. His love for the Father burns so strongly within him that he will go into the dregs of humanity and desire to become a part of the lowest of the lowliest.

As the prophet Isaiah foretold, he wills to be crushed as a worm beneath the cruel heel of this world that crushes so many other men and women. By a human choice, he freely wills to taste every ingredient in the bitter chalice that the world, in which the mystery of evil rules, can press to human lips.

The Father did not force Jesus. It is the Father's commands and wishes that lead Jesus to becoming the perfect mirror of the heavenly Father's complete emptying of self on our behalf. The Father awaits the free choice of his Son. He becomes surprised, pleased and happy in our historical time and space, because his beloved Son in human history does whatever pleases the Father. And the Father is pleased. In his infinite wisdom he himself would have chosen such signs of complete emptying, even unto the last drop of blood, if he had a body, if he could speak in human language of suffering unto physical death.

But he has a body! He has a physical presence in his Word made flesh. It is the Father who is speaking to each of us in the torn, mangled body of Jesus hanging on the cross, yelling out in the agony of being abandoned by the Father who loved him so much. "See, I have branded you on the palms of my hands" (Is 49:16).

Love unto death

In his service to the world, Jesus chose humanly to be like God by entering into the very depths of sin, death and utter emptiness of self. It was the most perfect way of imaging the eternal love of the Father for you, me and all human beings. We have no other way of knowing the Father except through the Son. Here we have the perfect expression in human language of the very being of God as humble love.

If God appears as love in the manger at Bethlehem, how much more does he appear as love in the stark poverty, humility and contempt of the cross? This act of freely choosing to be one with our sinful humanity, to receive the penalty for our sins in the most dramatic emptying, the *kenosis* to the death of the cross, is the most graphic act of loving service toward all of us human beings (Heb 5:7-10).

The emptying of the suffering servant of Yahweh had reached its peak in Jesus' death on the cross. God was being manifested for each of us as love, perfect in his self-surrender. "A man can have no greater love than to lay down his life for his friends" (Jn 15:13). And we might add, "Nor can God!" God reaches the peak of speaking his word, as humble love poured out on the cross through a pierced heart.

God-Trinity cannot be more present as love than in his image, Jesus Christ, made sin for us, rejected and outcast. In prayer, especially in the eucharist, you and I can realize with Paul: "For me he dies!" (Ga 2:19). Such an experience leads us into the awesome presence of the heavenly as perfect holiness, beauty and love. We realize that we are *now* being loved by our infinitely loving Father through the humble suffering servant of Yahweh, Jesus Christ.

Such a healing of our loneliness and proudful self-absorption bursts the bonds that keeps us in our narcissistic prison. It begins a transformation of our lives, which consists of a process of practicing humble service to others. "And the reason he died for all was so that living men should live no longer for themselves, but for him who died and was raised to life for them" (2 Co 5:15).

Humble service to others

As we experience this love, like Jesus we will *want* to live lives of self-emptying love, serving every person who enters our life. God is calling us to let his serving Word still walk this earth and go among the broken ones to bring them his loving presence through you and me.

To look on the face of a human being is to see a holy face. It is to see the face of *the* Son of Man himself, Jesus Christ. The image is defaced; but its beauty can be restored by humble, godly love, shining upon its darkness and bringing it into the glorious light of God's presence. Jesus, the *Ebed Yahweh*, lives in us, loves in us and wishes to serve his broken brothers and sisters through us.

Jesus wishes us to wash each other's feet (Jn 13:14-16). Humble, loving service to anyone—especially to the least and the smallest, the oppressed and the fearful, the lonely and the depraved—is the sign that Jesus is Lord and is redeeming us by freeing us from pride. We focus on God's word, revealing a Father who suffers as he serves to bring us into happiness.

Jesus, the suffering servant, still suffers as God's loving Word in the broken members of his Body. He speaks the words of the prophet Micah: ". . . to act justly, to love tenderly and to walk humbly with your God" (6:8).

Mary's Silent Humility

Love is incomplete until it is expressed in a humble, surrendering word that says: "I love you." Such a word, however, must be spoken out of an inner silence and humility and lived out by self-surrendering action.

As one star differs from another, so there are many different kinds of silence through which we express our need to love God and other human beings. There is the silence of two lovers who reach a union of love that silences all other words. All words are silenced before the silent approach of death. God speaks his word in the perfect silence of only one Word in whom all creatures have their being (Heb 1:1-4). There is the humble silence of the Word made flesh, as Jesus Christ gives himself to the Father on our behalf.

Perhaps God's silence, including the silence of his incarnate Word, Jesus Christ, is too much for us mortals to understand. We have ears to hear, but we fail to hear the intense, humble silence of the Trinity, which dwells within us and works lovingly in God's uncreated energies of love all around us. But in his loving providence, God has given us Mary as an archetype of what we are all called to become. We can understand her humility even better than that of Jesus Christ, since she is totally and exclusively human as we are.

Mary refracts for us in human experiences the self-emptying and humble love of God in the holiness of Jesus Christ. She holds out to us what we can hope to become by God's grace in terms of human growth. She stands before us as the first Christian. She is the first human being to become totally conscious that Jesus Christ lives in her and to surrender in faith and loving obedience to serve her Lord. As a pilgrim from the

82

beginning of her life to its end on this earth, she progresses further and further in her humble appreciation of God as the source of her entire being. She lives in "connected aloneness" with the Alone and thus becomes a bridge bringing all other created beings into the loving worship of God.

She is also the first-born of the Church. In her we see the Church as a collectivity of individuals in whom Christ's Spirit dwells, operates and produce his fruits of love, humility, peace and joy—signs of his active presence in the world. She is in a miniature form what the whole Church is destined to become by God's divinizing grace.

What she has been called to and has attained by God's grace, God also calls us to attain in every moment, by the help of the same grace. Karl Rahner makes this important point:

> God has eternally kept his eternal love in readiness for us too, so that in the moment that we call our baptism, he may come into the depths of our heart. For we too are redeemed, saved, marked with God's indelible seal. We too have been made the holy temple of God. In us too the triune God dwells. We too have been sent by him, from this beginning, into our life, that we too may carry the light of faith and the flame of love through this world's darkness, to the place we belong in his eternal radiance, his eternity.[1]

A pilgrim on a journey

Perhaps we have for too long conceived Mary's humility in static terms. This has made her "abnormally" holy and humble in a way that we could never imitate or attain. The Second Vatican Council well describes Mary as a *viator*, a pilgrim on a journey. Her growth in God's divine life unfolded, as she humbly cooperated with his grace and exercised faith, hope and love in the context of her concrete situation.

Like us she was in need of the redeeming grace of the only mediator, Jesus Christ. "Because she belongs to the offspring of Adam, she is one with all human beings in their need for salvation."[2] "She stands out among the poor and humble of the Lord who confidently hope for and receive salvation from him."[3] In each moment she had to discover God's immense love for her and humbly surrender to doing his holy will in all circumstances of her life. By the power of the overshadowing Holy Spirit, she had to become aware that God was her all, the source in whom her emptiness found fullness.

In her poverty and humility, Mary gradually grew in a surrendering adoration that was lived out by her fidelity to do at all times God's will. She silently listened to God's word and pondered it humbly in her heart. In the context of her daily life she lived in holiness, that is, she lived integrating all gifts of creation into wholeness. She grew into ever fuller degrees of grace by yielding to the promptings of God's Spirit and learning to silence her own words. Like us, she had to cooperate with God's grace at each moment of her life.

God as mother

Human beings are entirely sexual beings. Our sexuality is locked up inside each and every atom of our being. It exerts a response to God's daily call to enter into more intimate union with him and all created beings, especially all human beings who come into our lives.

Mary was the perfect woman, truly created in the image and likeness of God like all of us. "Male and female he created them" (Gn 1:27). If her femininity in some way images God, is it unthinkable that in her very physical sexuality as virgin and mother Mary experienced God as Woman, God as Mother?

At the annunciation and during the time of her expectation, God invited her to be as fully feminine, as fully virginal and as truly maternal as God is. Infinitely loved by God, she experienced a new sense, not only of herself as a woman, but also of God as being at once feminine and maternal.

She experienced God giving birth together with her to a Son through the Spirit. In mystical ecstasy she experienced the growth of the child within her from conception to birth. She grew from virgin to mother, from a state of receptivity to an ever greater fullness of grace.

She experienced the Spirit giving birth within her to something unique, re-creating her as a new person in God, enabling her to be spiritually born again on ever newer, higher levels of grace. She was filled with deeper humility before the condescending love of the Trinity working within her, which must have flooded her with an inner joy that can only be described by the word *contentment*.

Contentment is a state of being satisfied, fulfilled and at peace in total self-surrender to God as the source of all being. Like a child at its mother's breast, fully present to itself, yet fully caught up in a kind of ecstatic oneness with its mother. The past and the future are embraced in the nourishing, present moment. There is no fear.

Like a child full of awesome wonder, Mary knew that oneness with God, the source, being and goal of her existence. Her contentment in the Spirit describes her sense of being at home in God's protecting love, surrounded by God's maternal care and concern. All external and internal turmoil was dispelled by God's presence.

Living in the present moment

To surrender herself to God's will and to accept being the mother of the Word incarnate, Mary must have experienced God from early childhood as ever guiding her, protecting her as any loving mother would her child. She learned to penetrate each ordinary moment and to discover God inside its materiality. She quickly came to see how every created being she encountered was "connected" with the God in whom we all live, move and have our being (Ac 17:28).

"Commit your fate to Yahweh, trust in him and he will act" (Ps 37:3-5), became a way of life for her. Filled with humble, childlike trust, she found it easy to abandon herself with joy and peace to whatever God's will might be. Daily she gave thanks to God, her Mother and Father (1 Th 5:18), for all "bright and beautiful" things, which she accepted as gifts to her from on high. Because she found her strength completely in God, the source of all power, she was the happiest of all human beings. In her actual and spiritual poverty, she felt God's providence sustaining her, as a weak eaglet finds confidence to fly when supported by the mother eagle's wings (Dt 32:11).

If Jesus could relate to God as masculine ("My Father goes on working, and so do I," Jn 5:18), Mary could relate to God as feminine and thus develop an interior, profound hope. Hope was begotten in her as she confessed her own weakness. Such humility enabled her to trust in God's goodness and holiness. And it produced a reverence in her that made it possible to surrender totally to God's unfolding will.

> My soul proclaims the greatness of the Lord
> and my spirit exults in God my savior;
> because he has looked upon his lowly handmaid.
> Yes, from this day forward all generations
>   will call me blessed,
> for the Almighty has done great things for me.
> Holy is his name.
>
> (Luke 1:46-49)

She silenced a nagging voice in her heart that sought to persuade her to take control of her own life and to shape future events. How balanced she was, swinging from the present moment to embrace the eternal: "I am the handmaid of the Lord; let what you have said be done to me" (Lk 1:38). It is the feminine element in her—and in all of us—that is the unifying force in human living because it does not fear to surrender to Love.

Mary lived deeply in the silence of the present moment. And it was there that she found God's will speaking to her softly in his indwelling word. But most of us don't dwell in the present moment. We strain to embrace the future as *we* envision it, often to our own undoing. We drown out God's word, as we fill our hearts with the noisy clamor of our own designs for tomorrow. But our future depends on our humbly hearing and obeying his word in the grace of the present moment.

With great precision, Leonardo da Vinci describes the inner pull between God drawing us ever more intimately into his life and our anxiety about the future as we would wish it to be:

> Everything, everyone, wants to go back to the original chaos, like the butterfly that insists on being burned in the candle flame. Man is always longing for next spring, next summer, future months, new years. It always seems to him that the thing he lusts after never comes soon enough. Yet he never realizes that all he is asking for, in fact, is his own destruction, his own unmaking. And this desire, so unconscious and deep within him, is of his very essence. He has the spirit in him and this spirit, being aware that it is shut up in a human body, is always longing to get back to the one who put it there.[4]

Seeking the face of God in each event, Mary was able to discover a new incarnation in each present moment. We could say that God is again taking on "flesh," breaking into her world to pitch his tent near her, bringing his *shekinah* of infinite glory into the darkened world around her. Mary teaches us in

her inner integration that only in the present moment does
God meet us and bring us into new life in his word. Like Mary,
we too can with wonder embrace the presence of God in each
event and enter with her into the great adventure called life.
We are invited, as she was, to share in God's creative, loving
energies. We are called to co-create with him, out of the raw
stuff of each moment, the only real world there is, namely, the
world of living and loving in God's will.

Connected aloneness

Against the backdrop of a western world ruled by symbols
of masculine power like science, technology, aggressiveness
and rugged individualism, Mary stands as the symbol of the
eternal feminine. In her strong but delicate, humble but tender
obedience to God's holy will, she cries out to us that we
become truly human by first becoming truly feminine, dif-
fusedly aware of God's loving presence within and around us.
Only when we realize the "Mary within us," will the feminine
gradually develop in us and lead us to fully integrated per-
sonalities. Only then will we learn to let go of the conscious
control we hold over our lives and surrender them in inner,
humble poverty to God's gift of grace.

Mary knew how to focus. She was a truly centered person.
She progressively found God to be her center and source, the
one from whom she received her name and unique personhood. She lived in the "heart of her heart," that inner enclosed
garden where she mystically surrendered in love to the Bride-
groom of her soul.

> She is a garden enclosed,
> my sister, my promised bride;
> a garden enclosed,
> a sealed fountain.

> (Song of Songs 4:12)

In that Spirit-filled garden she knew her God. Her knowledge united her to him in the experience of a loving union. God's love, which overshadowed her in the silent, humble self-surrender of her being, bore the fruit of love. John of the Cross' beautiful words apply to Mary:

> She lived in solitude,
> And now in solitude has built her nest;
> And in solitude he guides her,
> he alone, who also bears
> in solitude the wound of love.[5]

Growth in freedom

It was Mary's humble silence which allowed her to live in such a profound openness to God's word of love. It was her silence which freed her to romp with him playfully on the mountaintops of ecstatic union. Because of her silence, she could truly make the words of Habakkuk the prophet her own: "Yahweh my Lord is my strength, he makes my feet as light as a doe's, he sets my steps on the heights" (3:19).

But to attain such humility through inner silence, Mary had to consciously strive to be attentive to the word of God that she pondered so faithfully in her heart (Lk 2:20, 52). Thus she experienced what Jesus himself had promised: "If you make my word your home you will indeed be my disciples; you will learn the truth and the truth will make you free" (Jn 8:31-32).

Mary is our model of true freedom, which is intrinsic to genuine Christian humility. This freedom does not consist primarily in being free to choose between good and evil. This is the lowest kind of freedom that we human beings experience.

There is another freedom to which God calls us and which Mary progressively attained. It helps us to experience, through the Holy Spirit, the *indicative* state of dignity that

God's free grace has bestowed on us. This understanding comes before we respond to God's call to keep his word. Then, in the light of our inner dignity, we are able to take our lives in hand and return them to God—love for Love.

The *imperative* which follows upon this realization and of which Paul so often speaks, is the peak of human freedom. Mary was perfectly free to love God. She did so neither out of fear or restraint, nor out of duty or a command of law. With her whole being, she recognized that she could not live without loving and humbly serving the Lord. She freely determined to live each moment of her life according to God's will. In so doing she knew that she would be the freest of all human beings. Living consciously in, with and for God through total virginal surrender brought her at each step of the way to a greater freedom, a greater desire and ability to allow God to be supreme in her life.

This does not mean that silence is equivalent to freedom. Silence is the preparation, the environment in which one can surrender to God's word and become free in loving submission to his will. Progressive appreciation and actual living in humble silence of body, soul and spirit relationships bring with them an awakening and awareness of the perfect love of God. Deeper serenity, peace, joy and stability of life result as the fruits of the working of the Holy Spirit within (Ga 5:22).

The strength of humble silence

There is nothing weak about silence. It centers us and gives us great inner power. In the life of Mary we see that, like Jesus, she too was tempted both from within and from without. In faith, hope and love she needed to turn in silence to the inner source of all strength. As we do, she had to struggle with the ambiguities of her daily situation and bring them under God's tutelage and wisdom in humble, child-like abandonment. She worried and suffered: "And his mother said to him. 'My child, why have you done this to us? See how worried your father and I have been, looking for you.' 'Why were you looking for me?' he replied. 'Did you not know that I must be busy with my Father's affairs?' But they did not understand what he meant" (Lk 2:48-50).

What temptations to despair must have assailed her as she stood silently at the foot of the cross before her dying Son! In that hour of utter darkness, Mary's motherly heart was torn in two at the terrifying sight of her Son's agonizing death. With him she passed from holding on to life to a complete giving up of life. With him she suffered the extreme physical pain and spiritual anguish of dying. She experienced in the very core of her being the truth of the prophecy of Isaiah: "The heart of each man fails him, they are terrified, pangs and pains seize them, they writhe like a woman in labor" (Is 13:7-8). She is asked to relinquish possession of her own life and to let go of the only thing that really mattered to her: holding on to Jesus as *her* Son. The *fiat*, which she had pronounced at the annunciation and countless times thereafter throughout her life, reached its full realization at the foot of the cross. Silence had prepared her for a theophany of God's love in the symbol of a pierced heart, from which poured forth blood and water to the very last drop.

Love for others

Love of God, begotten in humble silence, also begets love of other human beings. As Mary experienced God's love in prayer, she became progressively freer to love others by humbly seeking to serve them. Touching the Center of the wheel of life, Mary touched in loving oneness all the spokes that knowingly or unknowingly moved toward that same Center. She also knew the paradox that to be free is to become a slave to serve others in love. She knew that she was called to this service of others in love, and this was her greatest privilege.

We see her gentle concern for others at the wedding feast of Cana. This sensitivity to the needs of the guests came from her total silence on other occasions. She anticipated the embarrassment of the newlyweds by informing her Son ever so tactfully: "They have no wine" (Jn 2:3). Sensitive and totally feminine, Mary was open to the needs of all. Jesus learned from his mother how to be silent, humble, gentle, compassionate and loving toward all.

T. S. Eliot well expresses the paradox of Mary's silence that gives her the power to speak. He tells us of her emptyness that God can fill with the kingdom of heaven—of her being, in a word, authentically what God's holy will silently tells her to be when he speaks her name in his word:

> Blessed sister, holy mother, spirit of the fountain,
>   spirit of the garden,
> Suffer us not to mock ourselves with falsehood
> Teach us to care and not to care,
> Teach us to be still,
> even among these rocks.
> Our peace in his will
> And even among these rocks
> Sister, mother,
> and spirit of the river, spirit of the sea.
> Suffer me not to be separated
> And let my cry come unto Thee.[6]

Weeping for Your Sins

Christian prayer is adoration and worship of God as the supreme Being, the center of our lives. He alone is the Lord and is deserving of all our love. One aspect of authentic Christian prayer, however, is nowadays often overlooked. It is that of confessing our brokenness and sinfulness before the Lord in humility by God's power. This confession of our brokenness impels us to move out of our world of illusion and self-created desires, and into God's world of love, joy and peace.

Given more self-knowledge by the Holy Spirit, we realize that there is a powerful, negative force within us that influences our inner and outer behavior. We tend to deny this, since we know God as only positive and life-giving. In order to be healed, we must acknowledge this negative force, admitting that we really are sick and that we are not what we should be. We must receive God's grace, which summons us to awaken from our sleep, from a life spent in egoistic darkness. To receive such grace takes discipline and honesty. It requires an inner transformation to move away from our false self into humility; it requires the discovery by God's illumination of our beautiful, true self in Christ Jesus.

We can learn much by examining the early Christian writings on the spiritual life and prayer, especially those inspired by the Eastern Fathers and Mothers of the desert. These stress the necessity of being in touch with our own darkness and nothingness through a dread of being conquered by the enemy that lives inside of us. The Eastern Fathers called this process *penthos* in Greek. It was meant to be a constant element in all prayer, whether individual or public. They knew that sin in us prevents us from experiencing God's great love for us. That love is always active in our lives, but often we are dead to its presence. It can be experienced only when we honestly confess our brokenness, our inauthenticity, and our denial of God's goodness and love for us.

Isaac the Syrian expresses the common teaching of these early Christian writers and mystics of the desert:

> What salt is for any food, humility is for every virtue. To acquire it, a person must always think of himself with contrition, self-belittlement and painful self-judgment. But if we acquire it, it will make us children of God.[1]

Weep; there is no other way to salvation

One of the great graces I have received through my study of the Eastern Christian mystics is a deep conviction of the necessity to recognize our sinful condition. We must cry out for God's healing in a state of continual conversion. We must beg him to transform our brokenness into new life, as we turn to him, the source of all our strength. This is summarized succinctly by Abbot Pimen of the fourth-century Egyptian desert:

> Whosoever wishes to blot out his offenses can do so by weeping, and he who wishes to acquire good works can do so by means of weeping; for weeping is the path which the scriptures have taught us, and the Fathers have also wept continually, and there is no other path except that of tears.[2]

In the Christian West we all too readily think of sorrow and contrition for sins as an attitude that we must put on in preparing for the rite of reconciliation or during a retreat. But when we begin to live more consciously and more interiorly, we make contact with what Paul describes as "sin which lives inside my body" (Rm 7:23). Sin becomes something more than our deliberate acts of transgression against a divine law. The early Christian saints of the desert passed beyond the extrinsic aspects of the law, and we can learn much from them.

They had entered into a deep knowledge of their inner "heart movement" and a profound consciousness of God's immediate and tender love for them. Sin for them was anything that was an obstacle to joyfully living the good news of the paschal mystery. They experienced the same unworthiness before the awesome transcendent God which the prophet Isaiah experienced: "What a wretched state I am in! I am lost, for I am a man of unclean lips . . . and my eyes have looked at the King, Yahweh Sabaoth" (Is 6:5).

For one who lives superficially, such a confession of unworthiness before God has little meaning. But for those who with Paul enter deeply into their consciousness and even their unconscious, a whole inner world of fragmentation and darkness opens up. Perhaps in prayer you have experienced this inner duality as Paul did:

> I am unspiritual; I have been sold as a slave to sin. I cannot understand my own behavior. I fail to carry out the things I want to do, and I find myself doing the very things I hate . . . and so the thing behaving in that way is not my self, but sin living in me. . . . When I act against my will, it is not my true self doing it, but sin which lives in me. . . . What a wretched man I am! Who will rescue me from this body doomed to death? Thanks be to God through Jesus Christ our Lord! (Rm 7:14-25)

My sins are ever before me

In his writings Paul shows us how he grew in holiness by recalling his past sins to himself and to others, in order to deepen his spirit of compunction and contrition and to grow in humility. Along with so many of the early desert mystics, Paul found that the remembrance of his past sins did not breed a morbid sadness or a sickly introspection. It filled him rather with deep Christian joy and child-like confidence in the infinite mercy of God through Jesus Christ.

> I am the least of all the apostles, because I persecuted God's Church. But by God's grace I am what I am, and the grace that he gave me was not without effect. . . . I thank him for considering me worthy and appointing me to serve him, even though in the past I spoke evil of him and persecuted and insulted him. But he was merciful to me because I did not yet have faith and so did not know what I was doing. And our Lord poured out his abundant grace on me and gave me the faith and love which are ours in union with Christ Jesus. . . . Christ Jesus came into the world to save sinners. I am the worst of them. (1 Co 15:9-10; 1 Tm 1:13-15)

The more he realized God's infinite mercy washing away his past sins, the more he was filled with joy for being a forgiven sinner. His sins were ever before him, not because he was scrupulous, but because he had to distrust himself and put all his strength in Jesus. Jesus' grace alone made it possible for Paul to do all things in him (2 Co 12:9).

A self-created prison

When we do take time to move into deeper prayer, we also discover within ourselves two centers that vie with each other to control our value system. On one side there is the false ego or "kingdom of Mammon," which is fearful of and hostile to the outside world. It is proud, greedy, deceitful, guilt-laden, and has a sense of inferiority mixed with an aggressively attacking pride. The other center is the true self that has been made by God according to his image and likeness. This true self is noble, self-sacrificing, loving toward God and neighbor. It radiates humility, joy and peace in all its loving relationships with God's world.

The false ego is illusory. It has been created by our guilt and by our fear of not being loved by God and others. We create such an inner prison every time we move away from true love and enter into a state of self-centeredness. We build the prison and we are the prisoner. But we are also the jailer, who holds the key to open the prison door, if only we wish to do so.

It is above all God's love that shows us how tightly constrained we are within the prison of our selfishness and egoism. When we have the courage to turn within and in silence and honesty look into the tomb of our inner darkness, then the light of God's tender love illumines us. Ever so softly and healingly, interior tears well up in our spiritual eyes. We whisper in the depths of our heart: "Have mercy on me, O God, in your goodness" (Ps 51:1).

Authentic conversion

In such inner quiet we gently yield to the operations of the Holy Spirit, who shows us what needs continual healing from deep within us. We see our fragmentation, and we sorrow at seeing what could have been. We experience how great, tender and lasting God's love has been for us, but we also see our ingratitude and arrogance in turning away from God through prideful sins. We feel caught in a prison of darkness, and yet we can see a delicate ray of light leading us through the bars toward a conversion to the Lord Jesus.

We begin to experience our own inadequacies along with a burning desire to be set free from all falsity within us by the power of our Lord Jesus. The words of the prophet Joel take on a sense of urgency:

> Come back to me with all your heart, fasting, weeping, mourning. Let your hearts be broken, not your garments torn, turn to Yahweh, your God, again, for he is all tenderness and compassion, slow to anger, rich in graciousness, and ready to relent. (Jl 2:12-13)

As we sit within our interior desert, that is so much like the exterior desert of the athletes of earlier centuries, we learn to yield to the indwelling presence of Jesus, the healing Savior. He alone can bring life and give us that life more abundantly. We cry out day and night, distrusting our power to save ourselves, but with childlike trust in Jesus the healer: "Lord Jesus Christ, Son of God, have mercy on me, a sinner." This demands a life of reflection and sensitive knowledge of God's indwelling presence and infinite light of love.

In his light we begin to see our darkness and honestly recognize our guilt and sinfulness. We claim it as our own without justification or rationalization. We are broken and we need God's mercy. We have gone astray, and now our sins are ever before us! The spirit of compunction or abiding sorrow for our godless past and the fear of a future without God strangely enough allow us to humbly contact God. He truly does regard the lowliness of his servant! God gives himself to the weak, the poor, the needy. He looks with love upon the brokenness of his children, who have experienced that they are his created beings.

Inner resistance

In the spirit of our Christian liturgy, we fragmented faithful bring a broken world before a merciful God. We beg for inner healing of all that is false, proud and not loving. This is a vital part of our individual and communal prayer before God. It determines the depth of our true and effective conversion to the Lord.

The French Catholic philosopher Gabriel Marcel points out how we innately resist being converted from our false self to God our sole center:

> When we are at rest, we find ourselves almost inevitably put in the presence of our own inner emptiness, and this very emptiness is in reality intolerable to us. But there is more. There is the fact that through this emptiness we become aware of the misery of our condition, "a condition so miserable," says Pascal, "that nothing can console us when we think about it carefully." Hence the necessity of diversion.[3]

Such dread and existential anxiety cannot be removed without a complete upheaval and regeneration of our false selves by God's grace. In the deepest reaches of inner agony, that John of the Cross describes so well in his work, *The Dark Night of the Soul*, we wrestle with our nothingness. Our doubt assails our very integrity and religious identity. We seem to be lost on a dark ocean with no direction or light to guide us.

A proud person will not persevere in this inner strife of faith. He or she will rather seek to escape the darkness and feelings of nothingness by keeping busy and distracted, so as to perpetuate the illusion of being in charge. Dread divests us of any sense of self-importance. It cleanses us in God's Spirit from all remnants of a false world. We must experience this before we can live in God's real world of love and self-sacrifice.

Second movement in a true conversion

There is a second aspect of humility in any true Christian conversion. Our yielding to God's grace in our brokenness and our beginning to live a new life in Christ, result in a positive enlightenment. Initially, we stretch out to possess the new life promised us by God (Jn 10:10). The darkness within our hearts becomes light as we make contact with our Lord and Savior. His name Jesus, God who heals or saves, is on our lips and in our hearts. "If you will confess with your mouth the Lord Jesus and you will believe in your heart that God has raised him from the dead, you will be saved" (Rm 10:9).

The risen Lord Jesus releases his Holy Spirit, who in turn reveals that Jesus Christ, the image of the Father, loves you unto his passion on the cross. Paul's statement, "For me he dies!" (Ga 2:20), becomes an experience that leads you into the awesome presence of the heavenly Father as perfect holiness, beauty, and love. You begin to experience the integration of your frightened spirit, your scattered mind. Guilt and fear, anxiety and hatred, feelings of inferiority toward others as you attack them with unkind judgments, begin to dissolve in the tears of your own joyful reconciliation to God's immense love. You discover your true self in Christ for the first time. You enter into a "birthing" of your beautiful, unique person in the Logos made flesh, Jesus Christ. You feel as though nothing on the face of the earth, not even death, can ever take you from this intimate union with the Trinity through Jesus and his Holy Spirit.

Praying for the gift of tears

One of the consistent teachings of the Eastern Christian Fathers has been the need to constantly pray for the gift of tears. Evagrius of the fourth-century Egyptian desert writes:

Before all else, pray to be given tears, that weeping may soften the savage hardness which is in your soul, and, having acknowledged your sin unto the Lord (Ps 32:5), you may receive from him the remission of sins.[4]

This is of course a mystical gift that God freely gives; it is not absolutely necessary for salvation. But the desert Fathers felt that when a person was softened by years of such interior weeping, he or she would be more receptive to this gift from God. We also see this same gift in the life of many Western saints. Ignatius of Loyola wrote in his diary that for two years he would often weep to such an extent that he could not even read his breviary. Because of the God-given interior illumination of his nothingness and sinfulness, he only had to see the word "God" or "Jesus" and he would start weeping.

Effects of weeping for sins

The Fathers highlighted the greatest effect of compunction. It is the peace and joy coming from the love of God which the sinful individual who cries out for his mercy experiences. We should be able to appreciate this, even if we have not experienced it to the same degree as did those early great athletes of Christ. Purified of all inordinate, passionate desires, they knew a permanently abiding sense of tranquillity that begot interior happiness. This joy was not a result of the absence of trouble or blind resignation to God's providence. Nor was it a philosophical stoicism that ignores the rest of the suffering world. Joy was rather at the basis of their Christian experience: *per crucem ad lucem* (through the cross to light). Weeping with deep sorrow for our sins is the dying process. Joy is the resurrection of all our powers into a new life that produces a hundredfold in inner and even external joy.

One truth remains

Much in the writings of the fiercely serious early Christians of the desert is perhaps outdated and requires demythologizing. But one truth will always remain the same, both for them and for us Christians of the cybernetic society of the twenty-first century. We all need to be baptized by the Holy Spirit, received not once, but over and over, whereby we are always more washed of our own deep traces of resistance to God's love. But we receive this only if we cry out constantly for God's mercy in our great brokenness.

We are in continual need of God's recreating and healing love in our lives. Yet, God is always the forgiving Lover. He is ready to burst into our meaningless flow of consciousness in time with his meaningful presence. This allows us to make of the present moment of this *now* the eternal *now* of God's reconciling mercy. In our way we will experience what Jesus promised: "Happy those who mourn; they shall be comforted" (Mt 5:5).

The Practice of Humility

If there is one truth that Jesus lived by and taught his disciples, it is that love is proved by deeds. We can act lovingly by forgetting ourselves and living for the good of others only if our inner person is transformed into an integrated being. When we are thus made whole, we become ever more conscious of the Trinity's infinite love for us. Deeds then flow, not out of any obligation or for an ulterior motive, but rather out of our living at the core of our being. There, God's uncreated energies of love are ever actively loving us into persons who in turn love others as they love themselves.

Out of the same transformation effected by the Holy Spirit, humility likewise brings forth humble acts toward other persons in thoughts, words and deeds. The importance of genuine humility as the foundation of our spiritual life can therefore not remain solely in our intellectual understanding.

It needs to be enfleshed by our external actions toward God and neighbor. Thus, even these external actions are movements of the Spirit. They inspire us to "act" humbly and to influence our soul and spirit to grow even further in humility.

We need to go beyond any mere interior or exterior posturing as the Pharisee displays before God and the tax collector in Jesus' parable (Lk 18:9-14). Humility before God whom we cannot see is not authentic and transformed unless it is manifested in attitudes and actions toward our neighbor.

This is what Paul consistently taught.

Love one another warmly as Christian brethren, and be eager to show respect for one another. (Rm 12:10)

103

Love is patient and kind; it is not jealous or conceited or proud; love is not ill-mannered or selfish or irritable; love does not keep a record of wrongs; love is not happy with evil, but is happy with the truth. Love never gives up; and its faith, hope and patience never fail. (1 Co 13:4-7)

We must not be proud or irritate one another or be jealous of one another. (Ga 5:26)

Do not do anything from selfish ambition or from a cheap desire to boast, but be humble toward one another, always considering others better than yourselves. And look out for one another's interest, not just for your own. (Ph 2:3-4)

Be always humble, gentle and patient. Show your love by being tolerant with one another. (Eph 4:2-3)

Submit yourselves to one another because of your reverence for Christ. (Eph 5:21)

Learn of me, gentle and humble

Jesus insisted that we learn to live as he did. He was gentle and humble of heart before his heavenly Father and all who came into his life. He who was the master washed the feet of his disciples, his servants. He insisted that we do the same: "I have set an example for you, so that you will do just what I have done for you. . . . Now that you know this truth, how happy you will be if you put it into practice!" (Jn 13:15, 17).

Jesus gave us a new commandment of love that cannot be fulfilled without humility. "My commandment is this: love one another, just as I love you. The greatest love a person can have for his friends is to give his life for them" (Jn 15:12-13).

Here Jesus teaches us the intimate relationship between true love and authentic humility. They cannot be separable from each other, yet they are two distinct virtues. They are born of the same source, the Holy Spirit. Both give God complete preference over all else. Both come out of adoration, worship and reverence.

Love finds God by stretching out toward him. Humility meets God in the depths of our human lowliness. Both manifest total detachment from all created beings, only to find their true worth in God. The common aim of love and humility is to do all for God's greater glory.

"Love says: 'How beautiful God is!' Humility responds: 'Beside him, how vile I am!' Love says: 'See he is as good as he is beautiful. He takes no account of our littleness.' "[1]

First step to humility: true self-knowledge

Who we are before God and neighbor is determined by the quality of our thoughts, words and deeds. We come to know ourselves and how humble and loving we really are by understanding our interior motivation as we relate to God and to others in all situations. Not to know ourselves as objectively as God knows us, is to live in a world which our pride has constructed and which has no objective reality to its illusions.

This self-knowledge comes from the Holy Spirit's gifts of knowledge, understanding and wisdom (1 Co 12:8). We receive courage to see the good and beautiful that we bring forth as gifts from God. Yet, with our humble cooperation we turn all to God's greater glory.

But the Spirit first urges us to embrace those dark areas of our miseries, weaknesses and past sins and cry out for the healing power of Jesus, our Savior. He drives us into the desert of our hearts and calls us to a deeper conversion of our values to the values of Jesus Christ. Jerome dramatically expressed this truth: "Go into this dunghill of your mean and abject condition, of your sins and miseries; there you shall find the precious pearls of humility."[2]

Self-knowledge is the beginning and the necessary means to attain humility. For centuries the saints have proposed that we pray and meditate often to understand who we really are and have been in God's eyes. This understanding then helps us to increase in Christian love and humility in the future.

The saints also propose to understand our creatureliness by reflecting on our non-entity, our non-existence before we received the gift of life. God is the source of all existing created beings. We totally depend upon his gratuitous, creative acts, sharing with us the dignity to be made in his image and likeness (Gn 1:26-27). Paul also calls us to consider our nothingness in utter humility. He tells us not to pridefully think that we can exist without total dependence on God's gratuitous and creative power. It is God who wills us into being and sustains us in our existence. "If someone thinks he is something when he really is nothing, he is only deceiving himself" (Ga 6:3).

Sorrow for past sins

When writing on how to acquire humility, all Christian writers recommend the necessity to remember with deepest compunction and sorrow the sins of our past. Philotheus of Sinai well describes this consistent teaching of the early Fathers:

> Guarding the intellect with the Lord's help requires much humility, first in relation to God and then in relation to other persons. We ought to do all we can to crush and humble the heart. To achieve this we should scrupulously remember our former life in the world, recalling

and reviewing in detail all the sins we have committed since childhood. . . . This not only induces humility but also engenders tears and moves us to give heartfelt thanks to God. Perpetual and vivid mindfulness of death has the same effect: it gives birth to grief accompanied by a certain sweetness and joy, and to watchfulness of intellect.[3]

Jesus said that non-existence would have been better for Judas than to have betrayed his master (Mt 26:24). Yet each of us can see how many times we have been tempted and have succumbed with Eve to the temptation of being independent from God. God has been so good in granting us life and sustaining us for so many years, and yet how we have insulted God by rejecting his love!

We were all like men unclean, all that integrity of ours like filthy clothing. We have all withered like leaves and our sins blew us away like the wind. (Is 64:5-6)

Contemplating Jesus on the cross

We can humbly say with David the penitent: "For I am well aware of my faults; I have my sin constantly in mind, having sinned against none other than you, having done what you regard as wrong" (Ps 51:3-4). Yet, it is in contemplating the passion and death of Jesus that we begin to understand the evil of our sins. Jesus has freely accepted to bear them so that by his wounds we might be healed of our arrogant pride (Is 53:5).

Contemplating at the foot of the cross the Son of God suffering and dying, we develop a sorrow for our sins that is tempered and mingled with hope for pardon. We humbly cry out from the depths of our being: "Lord, Jesus Christ, Son of

God, have mercy on me, a sinner!" With Paul, we too can believe by the Holy Spirit that Jesus has died for us (Ga 2:19). And now we can accept God's forgiving love. We need no longer live in our pride but can live in Jesus-Savior (Ga 2:20).

Mark the Ascetic of the fifth century offers us the greatest reason for humility and the way to prevent prideful presumption with a true conversion from our sinfulness:

> All the penalties imposed by divine judgment upon man for the sin of the first transgression—death, toil, hunger, thirst and the like—he took upon himself, becoming what we are, so that we might become what he is. The Logos became man, so that man might become Logos. Being rich, he became poor for our sakes, so that through his poverty we might become rich (2 Co 8:9). In his great love for us he became like us, so that through every virtue we might become like him.[4]

Examination of conscience

There can be no true growth in humility unless we turn habitually within ourselves. Here we reflect in a loving dialogue with the indwelling Trinity on our motivation and value system that have been operating in every thought, word and deed in a given day. This is not an easy task. It demands daily attention, since our "false" self has built up over the years defenses insulating us from our true self, which lies deeply embedded within our unconscious.

In his *Spiritual Exercises* Ignatius offers us a simple but very effective form of a daily examination of conscience. It has been used world-wide by fervent Christians seeking to attain humility through self-examination. This exercise, performed at least every evening, contains five points:

1. The first point is to give thanks to God for the many gifts we have received from him.

2. The second point is to ask the grace to know our sins and to free ourselves from them.

3. The third point is to demand an account of my soul from the moment of rising until the present examination; either hour by hour or from one period to another. I shall first make an examination of my thoughts, then of my words, and then of my actions.

4. The fourth point is to ask pardon of God our Lord for my failings.

5. The fifth point is to resolve to amend my life with the help of God's grace.[5]

Through this simple exercise you will be able to move out into the material world and discover the *locus* or place of God's presence. You will be served by your transcendent self-presence to the Trinity in true, humble love. God has no mouth to speak, yet he speaks his word throughout all of creation. He has no hand to grasp you and guide you, but you know God touches you with his divine hand in the touch of each person whom you meet and touch each day.

Focus of attention

Another traditional exercise for acquiring humility is to concentrate in meditation and throughout a given day on a specific facet of humility, which you might feel you are in a particular need to develop. This is what Ignatius proposes in the exercise of the particular examen.[6]

An essential aspect in developing the habit of humility is to bring under God's will the basically good desire to entertain a just and right esteem for self and to be esteemed and praised by others. You can gradually develop this habit with the power of the Holy Spirit. You do so by consciously and affectively returning throughout the day to the indwelling Trinity, by renewing your resolve to do everything for God's greater glory, and by checking at the end of the day on your progress.

The best way to live humbly as Jesus did is to call to mind as often as you can throughout a given day the indwelling presence in you of the risen Lord Jesus. Perhaps you can recall this presence by using a breath-prayer such as, "You must increase; I must decrease" (Jn 3:30).

External signs of humility

The inner state of humility of Jesus and the saints is manifested through external signs. Before the majesty of God this occurred in prayer through bodily reverence. In relationship with others it is evident through their gestures, deeds and words. We realize how much the body can be not only the exterior expression of our inner humility, but also an influence on the soul and spirit, as we seek to *be* always humble before God and others.

We may be convinced of the importance of inner humility to fulfill the two great commands of loving God with our whole heart and loving our neighbor as we love ourselves. But we fear to practice humility externally. Basil of the fourth century says:

> As sciences and arts are acquired by practice, so also are moral virtues. To be a good musician . . . you must practise the art a great deal, and in this way you will come out

proficient in it. So also to gain the habit of humility and of the other moral virtues, you must practice their acts, and in this way you will gain them.[7]

Paul warns us: "It is not by hearing the Law that people are put right with God, but by doing what the Law commands" (Rm 2:13).

As we pointed out above, our bodies do influence the whole person on spirit, soul and body levels. Augustine explains this in the light of Jesus washing the feet of his disciples:

> But it is far better, and beyond all dispute more accordant with the truth, that it should also be done with the hands; nor should the Christian think it beneath him to do what was done by Christ. For when the body is bent at a brother's feet, the feeling of such humility is either awakened in the heart itself, or is strengthened if already present.[8]

If we are aware of Augustine's principle that bodily actions influence the soul, then our actions like washing the feet of travelers, washing the bodies of the sick in hospitals or homes, feeding the poor, the sick and the dying, can become sacramental signs of our humility, performing the corporal and spiritual works of mercy as Jesus himself did and preached.

> I was hungry and you fed me, thirsty and you gave me a drink; I was a stranger and you received me in your homes; naked and you clothed me; I was sick and you took care of me; in prison and you visited me. . . . I tell you, whenever you did this for one of the least important of these brothers of mine, you did it for me! (Mt 25:35-40)

There can, however, be the danger of hypocrisy in external practices of humility if these signs, gestures and words are insincere and instead of developing humility in us bring about more pride and self-centeredness.

Desiring to be abased by others

There are a number of difficulties in choosing external signs in order to either attain a higher degree of humility or to overflow a greatly developed humility. One of them is how to reconcile seeking to be abased, persecuted and ridiculed by others with having a proper esteem for ourselves and believe in the gifts God has given us to use them for his greater glory.

We must first realize that humility is not a static virtue—something we can suddenly acquire after doing certain "humbling" actions. Humility, much like love, must be seen as the process of our relationship with God, with other persons, and with God's other created beings.

I believe that Ignatius' consideration on "The Three Modes or Phases of Humility" in his *Spiritual Exercises* might help us.

In the first mode of humility we focus on the degree of generosity in our response to God's outpoured love in creating us. Ignatius writes:

> The first mode of humility is necessary for eternal salvation. This requires that I humble and abase myself as much as is possible for me, in order that I may obey in all things the law of God our Lord. Accordingly I would not give consideration to the thought of breaking any commandment, divine or human, that binds me under pain of mortal sin, even if this offense would make me master of all creation or would preserve my life on earth.[9]

This level of generous love and humility places God as the supreme source of my being. I would do anything to obey his commands as expressed in the Ten Commandments or avoid anything that would clearly take me away from living in his divine grace. At times this mode of humility might call for great generosity, even to the point of laying down my life for love of God. But it is also clear that at this stage we have not yet contemplated deeply the personalized love of the Trinity in the person of the God-man, Jesus. There are still areas of my life which I call "my own." God is real to a certain degree within the limited love-humility with which I respond.

The second mode of humility is more perfect and more generous, as my response to God now removes all boundaries that limit my generosity. I stand before God and seek to have "holy indifference," or in the words of Teilhard de Chardin, "passionate indifference."

> I am in possession of it if my state of mind is such that I neither desire nor even prefer to have riches rather than poverty, to seek honor rather than dishonor, to have a long life rather than a short one, provided that there be the same opportunity to serve God our Lord, and to save my soul.[10]

This mode calls for great humility before the allness of God in my life, so that I would not, "for the sake of all creation or for the purpose of saving my life, consider committing a single venial sin."[11]

The third and most perfect mode

Here we enter into a mystery of love and deepest union with Jesus Christ that only the Holy Spirit can give to us. We have progressed into purer love and humility over years of living, no longer we ourselves, but Christ Jesus in us (Ga 2:19-20). Ignatius expresses this most perfect level of humility:

This exists when, the first and second forms already possessed and the praise and glory of the Divine Majesty being equally served, I desire and choose poverty with Christ poor rather than riches, in order to be more like Christ our Lord. When I choose reproaches with Christ thus suffering rather than honor, and when I am willing to be considered as worthless and a *fool* for Christ who suffered such treatment before me, rather than to be esteemed as wise and prudent in this world.[12]

The folly of the cross

How can we justify such a degree of humility? It seemingly and imprudently is contrary not only to our personal instincts but even to reason itself. Does this not negate our basic goodness, always due to God's grace? Does God ask this of everyone? How can we even pray for such a generous humility and complete following of Christ when our entire nature resists the very thought?

Here we are entering into the essence of the suffering servant, Jesus Christ, who emptied himself of everything out of love for us, "to assume the condition of a slave. . . . He was humbler yet, even to accepting death, death on a cross" (Ph 2:7-8). How powerfully Paul grasped the love and humility of Jesus, who reveals it super-naturally to the little ones of this world:

> Do you see now how God has shown up the foolishness of human wisdom? If it was God's wisdom that human wisdom should not know God, it was because God wanted to save those who have faith through the foolishness of the message that we preach . . . to those who have been called, whether they are Jews or Greeks, a Christ who is the power and the wisdom of God. For God's

foolishness is wiser than human wisdom, and God's weakness is stronger than human strength. (1 Co 1:20-25)

We can see that humility is not only the test of the authenticity of all our Christian virtues, but it is above all the central condition of our transformation and regeneration into Christ. This mode of humility in no way denigrates our human nature. It surely did not do so for the human Christ. Paul saw Jesus' "emptying" of himself through ignominy and even abasement onto death, because Jesus was striving to image the face of his invisible Father. "But God raised him high and gave him the name which is above all other names so that all beings in the heavens, on earth and in the underworld, should bend the knee at the name of Jesus and that every tongue should acclaim Jesus Christ as Lord, to the glory of God the Father" (Ph 2:9-11).

The words of Dietrich von Hildenbrand well summarize the wisdom of God and of those who want to share in living this third mode of humility with Christ:

> The path that leads man to his ultimate union with Christ is not the unfolding of his natural powers and of the wealth of his gifts but his radical renunciation of self-assertion; the relinquishment and mortification of the self. "He who loses his soul shall win it."[13]

Need for prudence

If humility and love evidence the presence of the Holy Spirit within us, then the same Holy Spirit will also guide us along the path of prudence. Prudence brings balance between the two extremes: *excess* that lessens God's creation and his gifts in us, and too much *cautiousness* that all too often is a disguise for rank pride. As we prefer others to ourselves, prudence shows us that self-effacing humility does not change what we are but only what we seem to be through our sinful pride. It opposes anything that would diminish our personality and lower our moral worth. Prudence balances under the Holy Spirit a sense of beauty and justice, essential traits of true Christian humility.

Prudence also helps us to respect the individual calling of the Spirit and the various ways in which human beings can "live in Christ." Most saints desired self-abasement. Yet, we also find great and very generous saints who were apparently never drawn to imitate Christ in such a mode of extreme humility. Thus, not everyone will manifest the acquisition of humility in the same way. However, we need at least the desire to die to ourselves and to become one with the risen Lord Jesus. We need to be open to practicing that dying process unto transformation into Christ Jesus, in whatever way the Holy Spirit may lead us.

This transformation by growing in love and humility must be measured by our "magnificent obsession" to please God in all things as Jesus did, and to give pleasure to others by exalting God's gifts in them. This means to humbly love and concretely serve each person we encounter.

As we contemplate the greatness of God, not only in ourselves and in our neighbors, but throughout all of creation, we wish greater effacement of what does not belong to God, namely our nothingness and our sins. In this we miraculously contemplate the glory of God in his creation. All of us human beings have only one, true common aim: to give glory to God by seeking to please him in all things. His glory reigns throughout the universe. It is experienced by those who are gentle and humble of heart and have learned it from Jesus himself. Our constant, honest prayer, which will surely be answered by the Lord himself, should be: "Jesus, gentle and humble of heart, make our hearts like unto yours."

A Joyful Humility

Francis de Sales used to say: "A sad saint is a sorry sort of saint." And we could add that such a person would be no saint at all. We might even add that without a sense of humor, such a person would not be a highly developed and integrated human being. Could we ever imagine that Jesus lived without a sense of humor? If we do not discover Jesus being playful and humble of heart while not taking himself too serious, it may mean that we have lost our sense of humor and wonder before the heavenly Father. Have we perhaps made Jesus' humility according to our own image of what it means to be humble?[1]

We have already shown that humility is the right relationship of ourselves with God, with our neighbor and with all of God's creation. We also pointed out that pride is the most irrational, most primal root of all sin. Pride manifests itself in many forms of independence of God and others, as the false self glorifies itself in a conscious or unconscious turning away from God. Jesus lived a life of joyful humility, as he realized in every moment that the Father was greater than he and that without the Father he could do nothing (Jn 5:30; 14:28). All his power to preach, heal and perform miracles came to him from the Father (Jn 5:20).

He discovered the Father working in every detail of his life, and he joyfully played and worked in the Father's love and power (Jn 5:17).

> There in the depths of his heart, his innermost consciousness, Jesus touched the holy. He breathed, smiled, laughed and cried in that holy presence of his infinitely

117

loving Father. All outside created beings, touching Jesus in new, surprising experiences, were received by that delicate, sensitive gentleness in him as gifts. Absent were the moods of an angry, aggressive autonomy and uncontrolled self-indulgence.[2]

Rapt in the Father's presence

Jesus was constantly rapt in the loving presence of his Father, who poured his Spirit of love into Jesus' being. With joyful and humble response Jesus delighted to love his Father in each person he encountered. In each event he discovered the material to be gently received and to be transformed into love.

Jesus was consistently gentle, because he was at one with the loving Father. He knew his identity in the flaming love that the Father poured into his heart. He did not have to study other human beings in order to know how to act and react with gentleness and humility. He only needed to turn within himself. In the depths of his being he found his Father, bathing him with his uncreated energies of love. His nature was to be gentle, because that was the nature of his Father.

In that contemplative, worshipful attitude, Jesus lived and surrendered himself to his Father. He did not consider himself the sole criterion of all reality, but rather the Father's will. He was thus always joyful in the freedom he possessed to do all for the Father's greater glory.

Humor invites others to see problems and crises in proper perspective. Is it far fetched to think that Jesus smiled a bit in his loving gentleness toward the Samaritan at Jacob's well, as she coyly confessed to Jesus that she did not have a husband? Jesus replied lightly: "You are right when you say you do not have a husband. You have been married to five men, and the man you live with now is not really your husband. You have told me the truth" (Jn 4:17-18).

What humor Jesus must have shown as he looked up into the sycamore tree to unveil the presence of Zacchaeus and say to him: "Hurry down, Zacchaeus, for I must stay in your house today" (Lk 19:5). What joyful humility he showed, as he gathered around himself children to hug and bless them while his disciples complained to the mothers that the Master had no time to play with their children!

Humor and healing

In his book, *Anatomy of an Illness,* Norman Cousins describes how he was cured of a form of cancer through high dosages of Vitamin C and equal high dosages of laughter with his family, as they played games together and watched favorite comic movies. After he was healed, he lectured to medical faculties and medical students all over the world on the value of humor for maintaining health and bringing about healing of diseases.[3] He insisted that humor and a positive attitude toward oneself are powerful means to offset anxieties and stress that tear down our immune system and set up death-dealing sicknesses like heart attacks, ulcers and cancer.

Living under stress

We Americans are not a healthy people. One of the main causes is the stress under which most of us live. But an added fact is that we do not experience inner silence and healing of our bodily and psychological tensions by touching our indwelling, loving God as the foundation of our being.

Americans spend $150 million annually on laxatives alone. In a year we consume over 7,000 tons of aspirin. Tons of sleeping pills, tranquilizers, reducing pills and antacids are consumed, only to cover up symptoms and messages from a suffering, noisy body, flogged mercilessly by a disturbed psyche. Half a million die of heart attack, while 27 million have some kind of heart condition. Over 8 million have some kind of arthritis or rheumatism. One out of ten men have a stomach ulcer. Millions suffer from diabetes or hypoglycemia, chronic disorders as asthma, anemia, multiple sclerosis, cancer, senility, mental and nervous diseases, alcoholism, drug and respiratory difficulties. Twenty-five percent of Americans have a problem of obesity.

Dr. Hans Selye, the leading authority on stress, defines stress as "the body's non-specific response to any demand made upon it." You might be "stressed out" because of an argument in your family, a virus infection or a worry about your finances. Whatever be the source of our stress, physical or psychological, there will always be some bodily changes.

Our autonomic system reacts to such stressful occasions with the "fight or flight" syndrome. This is a surge of energy produced by the release of adrenaline from our adrenal glands. Your heart beats faster, your breathing accelerates. Your muscles become tense and ready for action. Whether the demanding situation remains objectively or only in our excessive worry or frustration, we enter into a prolonged high level of adrenaline pumped into our system along with other hormones that produce chemicals within our blood stream.

What follows is exhaustion and a lack of rest, which will produce chronic elevation of your blood pressure with slow but steady damage to your heart, kidneys and your entire cardiovascular system. This induces a tearing down of your arterial walls and increased plaque in your arteries along with raised cholesterol levels and lowered levels of an effective immune system.

Hope in the healing love of God

Is there any way to offset the ravages of stress in our lives? We Christians believe in God's infinite love for each of his children, especially in the healing power of his Son, Jesus Christ. We believe that Jesus went about healing the sick, provided they believed in his healing love.

Accepting such love in times of stress and trials will open us up to the transcendent presence of the indwelling Trinity within us. We humbly confess to God, the source of our being and without whom we can do nothing. And we humbly accept our human limitations and failures, our unloving, false self, as we seek to surrender ourselves childlike to God. Such abandonment brings us joy and peace and removes all "seriousness" that comes from false pride—as though we alone need to solve all problems and conquer all crises.

Father William L. Doty expresses how to overcome such self-absorption, solving our problems by seeking a proper, humble attitude toward God:

> We may even say that the person without inner humor is the person without inner peace because his disposition of soul is characterized by half-truth, lack of proportion and perspective, and unwarranted tension. Anxiety, for example, is a combination of these different factors. It normally results from an exaggeration of the significance of some particular trouble or threat to one's security, and it involves a failure to evaluate temporal difficulties in the light of eternal principles—a failure which in turn stimulates concentrated emotions of fear and stress.[4]

Humor and childlike trust

When we entertain a right relationship with God and neighbor, our mental "lightness" becomes habitual, radiating its joy to all our other emotions. It is rooted in God as the ultimate goal of all our striving. Even in suffering and infirmities we can rejoice as Paul did: "I am most happy, then, to be proud of my weaknesses, in order to feel the protection of Christ's power over me. I am content with weaknesses, insults, hardships, persecutions, and difficulties for Christ's sake. For when I am weak, then I am strong" (2 Co 12:9-10).

Such faith and trust infused by the Holy Spirit come to us by way of an intuitive knowledge and not by sole human reasoning. These bring transcendent values into situations of seeming absurdity or exaggerated self-pride. Without such simple trust and humility we will lack any humor and right consonance with the mind of God. If we expand our sense of humor beyond childish jokes and levity, we will experience God's will in each moment and our lives in proper perspective. Jesus and his disciples show us a sense of humor with God at its center through a childlike trust in him and a genuine humility. Such a sense of humor will enable us to discover joy, even in the midst of pain.

The gift of wonder

Both joyous humility and a sense of wonder are signs of children who enjoy an authentically balanced human existence that will bring a matured spirituality in adulthood. We increase our sense of wonder by believing in the mystery of God's humble but mighty love in each detail of our lives. We learn to surrender to his loving activities for us, as we open up to his uncreated energies of love.

Wonder helps us to enter into the mystery of love of God

and neighbor, and it always gives us a sense of surprise. We cannot by ourselves create wonder or surprise. But we can experience it in prayer. We enter into God's sacredness, as we move into awe and reverence before God's beauty and power, adoring in silent openness the divine maker of all beauty.

When we enter into the surprise of divine or human love we often feel uneasy since we are not in control of the situation. A new dimension of meaning is being revealed to us that challenges our habitual, rational understanding of being in control. In this uneasiness we ask new questions. New life is bursting all over the skies of our consciousness and unconscious, and we come alive with a new excitement in the presence of God as the source of all love. When we love one another, God's love is being perfected in us (1 Jn 4:12).[5]

Joyful humility and functionalism

Adrian van Kaam calls "functional seriousness" the chief ailment of our modern age.

> Our life of spiritual formation is the joyous presence in time of the eternal wisdom of God. If we lose this joyfulness, we become people without mystery. We trudge through this world like armies of ants. One ant cannot be distinguished from the next one. All of them follow the same functional line. Functional seriousness is the ailment of this age. We should ask the Lord to teach us again the art and discipline of joyful living.[6]

From God's view point the world is *one*. All created beings were meant to be inter-related in a harmonious wholeness, through the creative inventiveness and synergism of us human beings made in God's image and working with him. Each part has its proper place within the whole universe. Each being depends on and gives support to all the others in one great body, all of which has been created in and through God's Word (Ps 104).

Unfortunately, we have lost this memory of a life of harmony. But when we open ourselves in childlike simplicity to the working of the Holy Spirit, we recover the joyful humility that was given to the first man and woman before sin took it away and replaced it with pride.

Our joyful humility is the gift of the Spirit that allows us to walk again with new eyes of wonder and reverence before the transcendent God. This gives us the balance between seriousness as God's stewards and joyful humility. Obsessive seriousness as we try to succeed according to our self-centered understanding of success distorts our true values. As a result we measure our importance by our achievements, by our status before the world, by our power and possessions.

We can avoid an excessive lust of money, power and pleasures by balancing a true God-centered seriousness and a true caring for the concerns of our universe, with a cheerful humor. Then we can conquer any despair by trusting in God's goodness and mercy.

Finding God in the event of each moment

This joyous humility allows us to seek the face of God in the event of every moment. God is, as it were, again taking on "flesh," by breaking into our world to pitch his tent among us, to bring his *shekinah* of infinite glory into our darkened world. The historical time of this *now* moment (the *chronos*) is transvected by the eternal *now* of God's healing love (the *kairos*). God's grace in his uncreated energies of love touch our free will, and the body-being of his only begotten Son, Jesus, is extended again into space and time.

Not only will we find God in each moment, but we will also

seek to respond to his loving presence in each moment. The eucharist is God's gift of himself to us in his Son Jesus through his Spirit. Our daily lives are the "place" where we return our eucharistic gift of ourselves to God and neighbor. This place, this *now* event, is holy, for God's holy presence as love to us is unveiled there. It is holy because we respond by the power of the Holy Spirit to become God's holy children. This state of being is nothing less than *joyful humility*.

Humility in Suffering and Dying

We receive the greatest training in acquiring humility by accepting suffering throughout our lives. But we will have the most certain proof of our humility when we accept our earthly death not in a spirit of egotistic pride but in Christ-like humility. As Christians we are not to seek answers from Jesus to the perennial problem of suffering and death; he did not come to merely give us answers.

He suffered, as you and I do, not to be an answer to our problem with evil, but to become our *way*. Thus we move from suffering with Christ to sharing even now in his glory.

In his poem, "An Ode to the Setting Sun," written near the end of his life, Francis Thompson summarizes the paradox that one form of seeming death prepares for a new level of life:

> For there is nothing lives but something dies,
> And there is nothing dies but something lives,
>   Till skies be fugitives,
> Till Time, the hidden root of change, updries,
> Are Birth and Death inseparable on earth;
> For they are twain yet one, and Death is Birth.

Suffering unto new life

Jesus described the process of dying that is at the heart of accepting all suffering with faith, trust and love:

> If anyone wants to be a follower of mine, let him renounce himself and take up his cross and follow me. For anyone

who wants to save his life will lose it; but anyone who loses his life for my sake, and for the sake of the gospel, will save it. (Mk 8:34-35; cf. Mt 10:38-39; 16:24-25; Lk 9:23-24; 14:27)

He insisted that the grain of wheat had to fall on the ground and die, or else it remained only a grain. Only in dying would it release the great potential of bringing forth new life. Only by living out our baptism can we enter into the New Jerusalem. Only by a passover from slavery into the trials of our heart's desert will we share even now in God's life.

Suffering, trials, tribulations and our final earthly death are occasions to move beyond our proud, self-centered view of events and to open up to a faith-vision that the Holy Spirit can only infuse into the meek and humble of heart. Our prayer should be that of Soren Kirkegaard:

Teach me, O God, not to torture myself, not to make a martyr out of myself through stifling reflection, but rather teach me to breathe deeply in faith.[1]

Death, where is your sting?

Let us look at our final death, which ends our earthly journey, in the light of other forms of death-dealing situations. What we fear in these is to give up our pride that has penetrated into most experiences of our past life. There is self-centeredness in all our thinking, speaking and acting. We do not wish to even think about our final death.

The reason why we fear death is that as babies and even adults we fear to accept our human limitations. We fear that death would bring us to be separated from our loved ones. The reality of our death is a terrifying upheaval in our way of thinking, acting and living in general. It is a fearful sundering of the only existence we have known up to that moment. It is the most "unnatural" act that we have to undergo in this life.

Thus we learn not to think of death, and we deny that it will ever happen to us. We delude ourselves, thinking that we can suppress our fears and anxieties. Our western culture helps us in this death-denying process, just as it helps us to continue living in pride and self-arrogance. We believe that we are self-sufficient and therefore don't develop authentic humility that accepts our limited creatureliness.

The British historian Arnold Toynbee writes:

> Death is "un-American"; for, if the fact of death were once admitted to be a reality even in the United States, then it would also have to be admitted that the United States is not the earthly paradise that it is deemed to be (and this is one of the crucial articles of faith in "the American way of life"). Present-day Americans, and other present-day Westerners too in their degree, tend to say, instead of "die," "pass on" or "pass away."[2]

Death is everywhere

None of us can escape the ever-present reality of death in its various forms. We experience the constant process of dissolution in youthful growing pains as well as in middle age and in retirement. As we grow older, our parents, relatives and friends begin to die. Violence and death, so vividly portrayed in the mass media, are a constant reminder that we too will die. But since dying is portrayed as dehumanizing and impersonal, we block it out of our consciousness. The realization of our personal death is easily dimmed in the light of so many impersonalized deaths around us.

I believe that only the humble of heart will ponder their finiteness in a healthy way that calls them to new life. The proud do not wish to be reminded that they are not really the center of the universe.

In her book, *On Death and Dying,* Dr. Elizabeth Kubler-Ross presents five stages that dying persons usually pass through before accepting the "natural " aspects of death. These steps can also help in the process of dying to our self-centered pride and to reaching a state of humble, docile self-surrender to God in child-like trust. They are the folowing:

1) The dying person experiences an initial stage of shock and denial. 2) He shows anger and resentment toward loved ones, nurses, doctors and visitors. 3) Then he begins to bargain and sets up conditions to be fulfilled before he is ready to die. 4) The person becomes depressed. 5) Then he accepts the fact of imminent death.[3]

As in the process of developing humility, so also in accepting our final death or any "dying situation," we may stop half way and go no farther, or our final death may prevent the movement toward full, humble acceptance. Life contains a whole series of "death situations." We can be angry and resentful toward God because of what we think he is causing to happen to us against our own wills and desires.

We can even yield to deep periods of depression and despair. These attitudes, like those we may have toward our final death, indicate a need of a conversion or an inner healing. This healing is brought about by ever-increasing child-like faith, hope and love in our relationship with God and neighbor. Our degree of loving abandonment to God's providential care in life's death situations will be an indication of how we shall accept our final death.

Learning to be humble

Having examined the preceding chapters, do you think we can come up with an ideal way of teaching humility? If we could, do you think people would be as enthusiastic to learn about it as they are to learn how to make more money from the latest "do-it-yourself" seminars? We cannot learn about humility until we really *want* to. Usually we desire to know about something only when we have realized that we do not know about it. In the same way, we begin to desire humility only when we discover our limitations and turn to God as the source of all our power and goodness.

In this honest confrontation with our limitations and sins we realize the prideful illusions of our pseudo-power. We therefore desire to "die" to this illusory world by an inner revolution. Paul teaches us how to be transformed from death to new life in Christ Jesus:

> So get rid of your old self, which made you live as you used to—the old self which was being destroyed by its deceitful desires. Your hearts and minds must be made completely new. You must put on the new self, which is created in God's likeness, and reveals itself in the true life that is upright and holy. (Eph 4:22-24)

The death of Jesus

As a Christian you can understand the awesome mystery of death by prayerfully considering the death of Jesus. His death was his long-awaited hour, the baptism he had to receive. Great was his distress until it was accomplished (Lk 12:50). His death was a point in time, and it took place on a hill outside Jerusalem. But his death was also his entire life, as he strove to die to his own self-interests and to live in loving surrender to his heavenly Father.

Each moment of Jesus' earthly life was a preparation for his final death. Each choice was made in ever-growing freedom to place every thought, word and deed of his life under the good pleasure of his Father. He was in all things like us, save sin (Heb 4:15), for no one could convict him of sin (Jn 8:26). There was no injustice in him (Jn 7:18), because he always did what pleased his Father (Jn 8:29).

Jesus' human growth as a person consisted in the existential struggle for unity between his consciousness and the various levels of his unconscious. As Jesus learned to live humbly in greater interiority by centering all his thoughts, words and actions upon the indwelling Father, he learned to let go of the control he exercised over his own human existence. The temptations that he endured in the desert, as well as the agony of Gethsemane and on the cross, show us something of Jesus entering into an inner combat. He lived through an inner dying process to win the gift of freedom through a new victory of loving, humble self-abandonment to his Father.

As in Adam and in all of us, at the core of the temptations that Jesus underwent was the struggle between a state of independence from his Father and of free surrender in humble obedience to the Father's will. As for you and me, freedom for Jesus is God's gift through the Spirit of love. But it is won by a great struggle wherein the isolated self surrenders to the true self in freely given love. Without conflict Jesus could have experienced no growth into his full personhood in freedom, love and humility.

The kenosis of Jesus

Jesus did not suffer as a helpless victim who was passively put to death. His life was not taken from him; he freely gave it back to the Father with the maximum freedom, which showed the purity of his love for the Father and for all of us. When scripture says that Jesus descended into hell, it means more than what the First Letter of Peter 3:19 implies, namely, that he went to preach to the "spirits in prison."[5]

He chose to descend into the suffering, dying heart of humanity. He freely wished to become the poorest of the poor, the loneliest of all lonely human beings. By freely wanting to be so completely associated with humanity and God's created world that was groaning in travail (Rm 8:23), Christ speaks in that radical oneness with our broken world as the perfect image of the Father. The Father also wants to be radically one with us in self-giving, but can accomplish this only through his Word made flesh.

Our model before death

In the death of Jesus we find the model for all Christians who are faced, not only with their final death, but also with other death-dealing situations in their earthly journey. Jesus reaches his full human potential as he freely surrenders his life to the Father on our behalf.

He suffers the same biological pains as any other human being undergoing crucifixion. But he *actively* brings together a lifetime of free, loving surrender of his entire being to his Father. Nowhere as on the cross does Jesus enter into the fullness of his humanity in his free gift of self to the Father. And nowhere during his lifetime does he so enter into the fullness of his divinity, revealed to us as love poured out.

The glory of the cross

The secret of an authentic Christian death situation lies in the power of the cross. It is a logic and wisdom that go beyond the rational control of human nature. "The language of the cross may be illogical to those who are not on the way to salvation, but those of us who are on the way see it as God's power to save" (1 Co 1:18). Paul tells us of the power and the wisdom of God: "God's own foolishness is wiser than human wisdom and God's weakness is stronger than human strength" (1 Co 1:25).

The cross stands at the junction of our twofold identity. Here part the ways between the "natural" and the spiritual worlds. The cross also differentiates a Christian's view of death from that of someone not informed by the wisdom of God manifest in Christ. This wisdom is more than just logic or conceptual knowledge derived by human reasoning. It is an operative knowledge, which has power to change darkness into light, absurdity into meaningfulness, death into life.

Our whole Christian life should be put under the cross as Jesus himself insisted: "Unless a wheat grain falls on the ground and dies, it remains only a single grain; but if it dies, it yields a rich harvest" (Jn 12:24). Against the wisdom of the world he insisted that if anyone wanted to be his disciple and obtain eternal life, he had to begin by a "dying process."

Each of us has to enter into suffering, but this will deliver us unto a new life. We have to give up a lower level of self-possession that allows us to dominate and rule our life through self-pride. This means risking to surrender ourselves in faith to Jesus Christ and accepting his offer to move unto a higher level of existence guided by his Holy Spirit:

> If anyone wants to be a follower of mine, let him renounce himself and take up his cross and follow me. For anyone who wants to save his life will lose it; but anyone who loses his life for my sake will find it. (Mt 16:24-25)

Three stages of transformation

There are three stages in transforming our suffering and death and humbly accepting them as stepping stones to greater union with Christ and through him with the blessed Trinity.

The first stage, in the words of the early Fathers of the desert, is "to push the mind down into the heart." It is to enter into the "inner closet" (Mt 6:6) that Jesus spoke about when he instructed his disciples how they were to pray in his Holy Spirit.

This is a call to move away from our carnal-minded pride and to enter into the transcendental presence of the indwelling Trinity. It is in this place of the *heart* that we are to meet the risen Jesus. There he reveals through his Spirit's faith that this suffering and even death can truly work for our good as "God co-operates with all those who love him" (Rm 8:28).

But how we dread entering into our innermost selves! We fear that we might have to trust in God alone and destroy in our mind the idols of a God who can never be called by name. Only in inward silence can we hear God speak new meaning into suffering. Such inner solitude engenders humility when we learn to leave the flattering, pampering world of the senses and illusions. It comes about only if we have the courage to taste our inner poverty in and through humility.

The second stage comes from our being forced to ask ourselves, "Who am I?" This question forces us in our brokenness, sinfulness and "zero-ness" to give meaning to such illogical things as suffering, trials and death itself, in order to confront who Jesus Christ really is for us.

Consequently, faith becomes a response to his invitation to suffer with him, in order to enter into union with him even now and to live in his glorified, resurrectional life. It is to know by faith and experience what our personal sinfulness and frailty mean; what it means to have spurned, in the folly of our arrogant pride, the infinite love of God given to us through Jesus Christ, who has died out of humble love for us. It is to confront our inauthentic selves, covered by the hard shell of our self-containment or pride.

We weep and mourn for our blindness, which leads us to the third stage: to bring about humility. By consecrating our suffering through faith, we sublimate it and live it with child-like trust in the power of the risen Lord. Thus we enter into a deeper union with Christ as proof that God truly exalts the humble.

Give praise to the Lord

The sign of our new relationship with the Trinity is our readiness to praise God in all circumstances. We Christians learn through the Holy Spirit's infusion of faith, hope and love, how to praise God in all seasons. In everything that happens to us God is loving us and showering upon us the gift of himself. Praise is what flows from the depths of our being, as we surrender lovingly to him.

Paul and Silas prayed and sang praises to God from their prison cell. We too can through humility raise our hands, even when suffering bows us down to the earth, and pray, "We give thanks to God and the Father of our Lord Jesus Christ." Adversities allow us to humble ourselves before God so that he may raise us up to a new union of love with him (1 Pt 5:6-7).

Here is the true proof of our humility: When humility and love meet in us through Jesus Christ and give us freedom through the Holy Spirit to rejoice in our infirmities and weaknesses; when Christ is our strength and in him we can do all things (2 Co 12:9-10). Then we too can pray with Paul in deepest humility and love:

> We know that by turning everything to their good God co-operates with all those who love him, with all those that he has called according to his purpose. . . . After saying this, what can we add? With God on our side who can be against us? Since God did not spare his own Son, but gave him up to benefit us all, we may be certain, after such a gift, that he will not refuse anything he can

give. . . . Nothing therefore can come between us and the love of Christ, even if we are troubled or worried, or being persecuted, or lacking food or clothes, or being threatened or even attacked. . . . These are the trials through which we triumph, but by the power of him who loved us. For I am certain of this: neither death nor life, nor angel, nor prince, nothing that exists, nothing still to come, not any power, or height or depth, nor any created thing, can ever come between us and the love of God made visible in Christ Jesus our Lord. (Rm 8:28-39)

Notes

Introduction

1. Augustine of Hippo, *On Holy Virginity*, Nicene and Post-Nicene Fathers, 1st series, ed. P. Schaff (Peabody: Hendrickson Publishers, 1994), 3:43.
2. Charles Taylor, *Sources of the Self—The Making of the Modern Identity* (Cambridge, 1985), 32.
3. Ted Turner, *The Meaning of Life*, ed. David Friend and the editors of *Life Magazine* (Boston: Time-Life Company, 1991), 73.
4. T. S. Eliot quoted in Robert J. Furey, *So, I'm Not Perfect—A Psychology of Humility* (Staten Island: Alba House, 1986), 10.

Whatever Happened to Humility?

1. Victor E. Frankl, *La psychotherapie et son image de l'homme* (Paris, 1970), 150.
2. Emil Brunner, *Man in Revolt* (London: Lutterworth Press, 1953), 98.
3. Malachi Martin, *Jesus Now* (New York: E. P. Dutton and Co., 1973), 5-20.
4. Thomas à Kempis, *The Imitation of Christ* (New York: Marcel Rodd Co., 1945), 87.
5. Willard Gaylin, *Feelings* (New York, 1979), 77.
6. Furey, *So, I'm Not Perfect*, 17-18.
7. Samuel Dresner, S.J., *Three Paths of God and Man* (New York: Sheed and Ward, 1960), 57.
8. Karl Menninger, *Whatever Became of Sin?* (New York: Hawthorn Books, 1973), 13.
9. Dorotheos of Gaza, *Discourses and Sayings*, tr. Eric P. Wheeler (Kalamazoo: Cistercian Publications, 1977), 144.
10. John Paul II, *The Splendor of Truth*, in *Origins*, vol. 23, n. 18 (Washington: CNS Documentary Services, 1993).
11. *The Catholic Encyclopedia* (New York: Robert Appleton Co., 1910), 7:543.
12. Thomas Aquinas, *Summa Theologica* (New York: Benziger Brothers, Inc., 1947), 2:1848.
13. Thomas Aquinas, *Contra Gentes*, tr. J. Rickaby, S.J. (New York: Benziger Brothers, Inc., 1947), 210.
14. Abraham Maslow, *Motivation and Personality* (New York: Harper and Brothers, 1970), 83.

The Nature of True Humility

1. John Climacus, *The Ladder of Divine Ascent*, tr. Colm Luibheid and Norman Russell (New York: Paulist Press, 1982), 218-19.
2. Climacus, *Ladder of Divine Ascent*, 219.
3. See P. Adnes, S.J., *Dictionnaire de Spiritualité* (Paris, 1969), 7:1136-87.
4. Joseph de Guibert, S.J., *The Theology of the Spiritual Life*, tr. Paul Barrett, O.F.M. Cap. (New York: Sheed and Ward, 1953).
5. John Cassian, *Institutes*, cited in de Guibert, *Theology of the Spiritual Life*, 279.
6. Gregory the Great, cited in de Guibert, *Theology of the Spiritual Life*, 279.
7. Gillian R. Evans, tr., *Bernard of Clairvaux—Selected Works* (New York: Paulist Press, 1987), 103.
8. Aquinas, *Summa Theologica*, 1:1848.
9. Aquinas, *Summa Theologica*, 1:1849.
10. Aquinas, *Summa Theologica*, 1:1850.
11. Aquinas, *Summa Theologica*, 1:1854ff.
12. Cf. Climacus, *The Ladder of Divine Ascent*, 218ff.
13. Cf. Dietrich von Hildebrand, *Transfiguration in Christ* (New York: Longmans, Green and Co., 1950).
14. Aquinas, *Summa Theologica*, 1:1851.
15. Rudolf Otto, *The Idea of the Holy*, tr. John W. Harvey (New York: Oxford University Press, 1958), 5-11.
16. Augustine of Hippo, *Sermon 69*, Patrologia Latina, ed. Migne (Paris, undated), 38:441.

The Spirituality of the Anawim of God

1. Johannes Metz, *Poverty of Spirit*, tr. John Drury (Paramus: Paulist Press, 1968), 26.

Jesus' Teaching on Humility

1. Metz, *Poverty of Spirit*, 38.

Jesus, Humble Servant

1. See Raymond E. Brown, *Jesus God and Man* (Milwaukee: Bruce Publishers, 1967); Jacques Gillet, S.J., *The Consciousness of Jesus* (New York: Sheed and Ward, 1972); Piet Schoonenberg, S.J., *The Christ* (New York: Herder and Herder, 1971).

Mary's Silent Humility

1. Karl Rahner, S.J., *Mary, Mother of the Lord* (New York: Sheed and Ward, 1963), 49.
2. *Constitution on the Church*, #52, in *Second Vatican Council—The Conciliar*

and Post Conciliar Documents, ed. Walter M. Abbott, S.J. (New York: America Press, 1966).

3. *Constitution on the Church,* #55.

4. Leonardo da Vinci cited in E. Danniel and B. Olivier, *Woman is the Glory of Man* (Westminster: Newman, 1966).

5. John of the Cross, *Spiritual Canticle,* stanza 35, in *The Collected Works of Saint John of the Cross,* tr. Kieran Kavanaugh and Otilio Rodriguez (Washington: ICS Publications, 1973), 543.

6. T. S. Eliot, "Ash Wednesday," in *The Four Quartets* (New York: Harcourt, Brace and World, Inc., 1943), 98.

Weeping for Your Sins

1. Isaac the Syrian, *Directions on Spiritual Training* #100, The Philokalia: Early Fathers, ed. and tr. George Palmer et al. (London: Faber and Faber, 1954), 210-11.

2. Abbot Pimen cited in W. Budge, *The Wit and Wisdom of the Christian Fathers of Egypt* (London: Oxford University Press, 1934), 44.

3. Gabriel Marcel, *The Problematic Man* (Chicago: H. Regnery Co., 1961), 100.

4. Evagrius, *De Oratione,* Patrologia Graeca, 79:1168D.

The Practice of Humility

1. Louis Beaudenom, *The Path of Humility* (Baltimore: Helicon, 1950), 282.

2. Jerome cited in Alphonse Rodriguez, S.J., *The Practice of Perfection and Christian Virtues,* tr. Joseph Rickaby, S.J. (Chicago: Loyola Press, 1929), 2:190.

3. Philotheus of Sinai, *Forty Texts on Watchfulness* #3, The Philokalia: Early Fathers, 20.

4. Mark the Ascetic, *Letter to Nicolas the Solitary* #1, The Philokalia: Early Fathers, 155.

5. Ignatius of Loyola, *The Spiritual Exercises,* tr. Anthony Mottola (Garden City: Doubleday Image Books, 1964), 53.

6. Ignatius, *Spiritual Exercises,* 48-49.

7. Basil cited in Rodriguez, *Practice of Perfection and Christian Virtues,* 261.

8. Augustine of Hippo, *On the Gospel of St. John,* Nicene and Post-Nicene Fathers, 1st series, 7:306.

9. Ignatius, *Spiritual Exercises,* 81-82.

10. Ignatius, *Spiritual Exercises,* 82.

11. Ignatius, *Spiritual Exercises,* 82.

12. Ignatius, *Spiritual Exercises,* 82.

13. von Hildenbrand, *Transfiguration into Christ,* 154.

A Joyful Humility

1. See my book, *That Your Joy May Be Complete* (Hyde Park: New City Press, 1994), 28ff.
2. Maloney, *That Your Joy May Be Complete*, 32.
3. Norman Cousins, *An Anatomy of an Illness* (New York: Doubleday, 1968).
4. See William L. Doty, *Pathways to Personal Peace* (St. Louis: Herder and Herder, 1965), 129.
5. See my book, *Deep Calls to Deep—A Christian Spirituality of the Heart* (Denville: Dimension Books, 1993), 25ff.
6. Adrian van Kaam, C.S.Sp., *The Roots of Christian Joy* (Denville: Dimension Books, 1985), 110ff.

Humility in Suffering and Dying

1. Perry D. Lefevre, ed., *The Prayers of Soren Kierkegaard* (New York: Paulist Press, 1975), 36.
2. Arnold Toynbee et al., *Man's Concern with Death* (New York: McGraw-Hill, 1969), 131
3. Elizabeth Kubler-Roth, *On Death and Dying* (New York: Macmillan Co., 1969), 34ff.
4. On this point see Karl Rahner, *On the Theology of Death*, tr. Charles H. Henkey (New York: Herder and Herder, 1961), 72-73.

Select Bibliography

Aquinas, Thomas. *Summa Theologica*. New York: Benziger Brothers, Inc., 1947.

Beaudenom, Louis. *The Path of Humility*. Baltimore, 1950.

Bergamo, Cajetan da. *Humility of the Heart*. Westminster, 1944.

Bondi, Roberta. *To Love As God Loves*. Philadelphia, 1987.

Canice, Fr. *Humility—The Foundation of the Spiritual Life*. Westminster: Newman Press, 1995.

Carlson, S. *The Virtue of Humility*. Dubuque, 1952.

Climacus, John. *The Ladder of Divine Ascent*. New York, 1982.

Doty, William. *Pathway to Personal Peace*. St. Louis: Herder and Herder, 1965.

Dresner, Samuel. *Three Paths of God and Man*. New York: Sheed and Ward, 1960.

Evans, Gillian et al., ed. and tr., *Bernard of Clairvaux—Selected Works*. New York: Paulist Press, 1987.

Furey, Robert J. *So, I'm Not Perfect—A Psychology of Humility*. Staten Island: Alba House, 1986.

Guibert, Joseph de. *The Theology of the Spiritual Life*. Translated by Paul Barrett. New York: Sheed and Ward, 1953.

Hildenbrand, Dietrich von. *Transfiguration into Christ*. New York: Longmans, Green and Co., 1955.

Ignatius of Loyola, *The Spiritual Exercises*. Translated by Anthony Mottola. Garden City: Doubleday Image Books, 1964.

Kaam, Adrian van. *The Roots of Christian Joy*. Denville: Dimension Books, 1985.

Kempis, Thomas à. *The Imitation of Christ*. New York: Marcel Rodd Co., 1988.

Kinsella, N. *Unprofitable Servants*. Westminster: Newman, 1960.

Maloney, George A. *Deep Calls to Deep—A Christian Spirituality of the Heart*. Denville: Dimension Books, 1993.

_____. *Pilgrimage of the Heart—A Treasury of Eastern Christian Spirituality*. San Francisco: Harper and Row, 1983.

141

_____. *That Your Joy May Be Complete.* Hyde Park: New City Press, 1994.

Menninger, Karl. *Whatever Became of Sin?* New York: Hawthorn Books, 1973.

Murray, Andrew. *Humility: The Beauty of Holiness.* Old Tappan, undated.

Palmer, George, et al., ed. and tr. *The Philokalia: Early Fathers.* Vols. 1-3. London-Boston: Faber and Faber, 1986.

Rodriguez, Alphonse. *Practice of Perfection and Christian Virtues.* Vol. 2. Translated by Joseph Rickaby. Chicago: Loyola Press, 1929.

Schoonenberg, P. *Man and Sin.* Translated by J. Donceel. Notre Dame: Ave Maria Press, 1965.

Wright, Wendy M., and Joseph F. Power, eds., *Francis de Sales, Jane de Chantal—Letters of Spiritual Direction.* New York: Paulist Press, 1988.

That Your Joy May Be Complete
The Secret of Becoming a Joyful Person

"Is there a single person who does not wish for more joy in life? Maybe the reason joy is in short supply is that we equate it with pleasure and forget that it is a gift of the Holy Spirit. Fr. Maloney reminds us of the true Source, and shows how authentic Christian joy is a sign of the indwelling Trinity gifting us with the eternal joy of the divine community."

Book Nook

ISBN 1-56548-062-7, **2d printing**
paperback, 5 3/8 x 8 1/2, 144 pp.

God's Community of Love
Living in the Indwelling Trinity

"[The author's] introduction to life in the Trinity begins with four chapters which rely on Scripture, mystical theologians of Eastern and Western Christian theology, and the mystics themselves to describe the inner life of the Trinity. Then five chapters deal with 'the loving relationships of the three-personed God in their created world.' "

Theology Digest

ISBN 1-56548-024-4, **2d printing**
paperback, 5 3/8 x 8 1/2, 144 pp.